KIDBIZ

Everything You Need to Start Your Own Business

BY CONN MCQUINN
ILLUSTRATED BY MIKE REDDY

PUFFIN BOOKS

PUFFIN BOOKS
Published by the Penguin Group
Penguin Putnam Books for Young Readers, 345 Hudson Street, New York, New York 10014, U.S.A.
Penguin Books Ltd, 27 Wrights Lane, London W8 5TZ, England
Penguin Books Australia Ltd, Ringwood, Victoria, Australia
Penguin Books Canada Ltd, 10 Alcorn Avenue, Toronto, Ontario, Canada M4V 3B2
Penguin Books (N.Z.) Ltd, 182-190 Wairau Road, Auckland 10, New Zealand

Penguin Books Ltd, Registered Offices: Harmondsworth, Middlesex, England

First published in the United States of America by Puffin Books,
a member of Penguin Putnam Books for Young Readers, 1999

1 3 5 7 9 10 8 6 4 2

KidBiz is produced by becker&mayer!, Kirkland, Washington.
www.beckermayer.com
Spreadsheet production by Dwayne Broome

LIBRARY OF CONGRESS CATALOGING-IN-PUBLICATION DATA
McQuinn, Conn.
Kidbiz : everything you need to start your own business / Conn McQuinn ; illustrated by Mike Reddy.
p. cm.
"Windows compatible"—T.p. verso.
Includes bibliographical references.
Summary: Offers advice for young people interested in starting their own business and describes
thirty possible ideas, from car washing and lawn mowing to giving children's parties
and making jewelry. Includes computer spreadsheet program and templates for various forms.
ISBN 0-14-038811-7 (pbk.)
1. Money-making projects for children—Juvenile literature. 2. New business enterprises—Juvenile literature.
3. Entrepreneurship—Juvenile literature. 4. Business—Computer programs—Juvenile literature.
5. Electronic spreadsheets—Juvenile literature. 6. Business—Forms—Computer programs—Juvenile literature.
[1. Moneymaking projects. 2. Business enterprises. 3. Entrepreneurship.] I. Reddy, Mike, ill. II. Title.
HF5392.M35 1999 650.1'4—dc21 97-49142 CIP AC

Printed in the United States of America

To Alec and Caitlin, who are always
giving me the business, and to Fred and Jan,
the best in-laws this side of Terre Haute
—C.M.

For my parents
—M.R.

CONTENTS

Note to KIDS

Before starting up your own business, you should consult with your parents to get their support. Once you have their approval, it will be easier to ask them and other adults you know for help and advice. You may want to borrow equipment from them, too! If your parents are not sure they should let you start your own business, show them the note on the next page.

Note to Parents

Be supportive! There are no guarantees of financial success, but your kids will learn responsibility, organizational skills, and effective communication techniques. They will learn how to handle money, and they may develop a hobby or discover a talent that can be theirs for a lifetime. They need your encouragement, your advice, and your help.

I have attempted to make sure that the ideas and projects in this book are legal, appropriate, and safe. However, you should check to make certain that your kids are not violating any local zoning, business, or tax laws in running their own businesses. You should also assist your kids as they plan and operate their businesses, in order to avoid practices and situations that might be unsafe.

Some of the businesses described in this book are more difficult than others. They may not be appropriate for younger children. Do not let young children use tools such as a hammer or saw without supervision. Caution them not to go into a stranger's house. They can and should bring their business to family members, friends, and personal references—not strangers. In addition, your child may need guidance to handle larger amounts of cash than he or she is accustomed to. Use your common sense to avoid problems and encourage your kids to do the same.

KIDBIZ

SO YOU WANT TO START A BUSINESS!

Many kids across the country are operating their own businesses. If you talk to adults who run successful companies, you often find that they started their first businesses when they were kids! Successful businesses run by kids include snow shoveling, desktop publishing, making customized T-shirts, and many, many more.

Why do people sell lemonade, design T-shirts, or run a tutoring business? Because it's an exciting challenge! It's a chance to take a creative idea, combine it with work and skill, and create a successful enterprise. And you can make some money, too!

BUT is starting a business something that you really want to do? Let's look at the advantages and disadvantages of running your own business.

ADVANTAGES

- It can be fun!
- You can spend time doing something you really enjoy.
- You will learn new skills that will be useful for the rest of your life.
- You can meet a lot of interesting people.
- You can earn money!

DISADVANTAGES

- It's a lot of work.
- It takes careful planning and organization to be successful.
- You often have to work on weekends, or before and after school.

There's a reason why I didn't mention earning money at the top of the Advantages list. First of all, it's quite possible that you won't earn a lot of money. Starting a business is no sure thing, and there's always a chance that you will have to give it up and try again.

SO, IF MONEY ISN'T THE REASON WHY DO IT?

Why try to hit home runs? Why play the piano? Why try to beat video game monsters? Because it's a challenge. It's a chance for you to choose a goal and to pursue it to the best of your ability. And by reaching for that goal, you'll learn more every day about yourself and about stretching your skills. (Don't tell anyone, but there's even a good chance it will improve your grades in school.)

And of course, it doesn't hurt to earn a few bucks, either!

Things I'll Buy with My Earnings!

1. New bike
2. Comic books
3. CDs
4. Baseball mitt
5. Pizza
6. Sneakers
7. Posters
8. Movie tickets
9. Ice cream sundaes
10. Basketball

What will *you* buy? Make your own list of rewards.

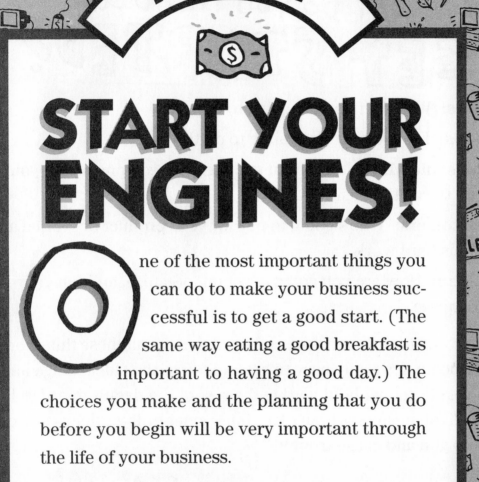

PART 1

START YOUR ENGINES!

One of the most important things you can do to make your business successful is to get a good start. (The same way eating a good breakfast is important to having a good day.) The choices you make and the planning that you do before you begin will be very important through the life of your business.

WHAT DO YOU NEED to GET STARTED?

Ideas: What is it you are going to do?

Skills: Do you have the ability to do the job?

Tools and Materials: What supplies and equipment will you need to run the business?

Customers: Who's going to pay for your product or service after all this hard work?

A Plan: How are you going to set up, organize, and run your enterprise?

For a business to succeed, you need to have all these things before you begin. It's really easy to get excited at the "Idea" stage and try to get started without getting the rest of the details in order. Don't do it! You might start out okay, but sooner or later things will catch up to you and cause trouble.

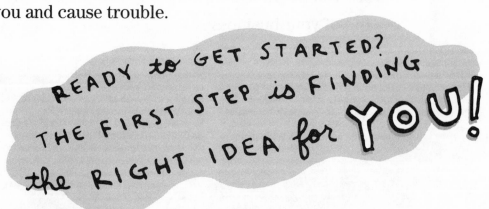

READY to GET STARTED? THE FIRST STEP is FINDING the RIGHT IDEA for YOU!

IDEAS!

What kinds of businesses are there?

When you get right down to it, there are just two basic kinds of businesses: *services* and *products*. A service business involves doing a service for someone—such as mowing the lawn. A product business is one in which you sell a product—such as a glass of lemonade.

SERVICE BUSINESSES

If you start a service business, then you need to have a skill that customers are willing to pay for. That may not be hard to find. There are lots of jobs out there that adults are too busy to do, or just plain tired of doing themselves. Some advantages of service businesses are that they often don't take much money to start, and usually the service (such as lawn mowing) is something that the customers need over and over again.

A disadvantage of a service business is that you have to work when it's convenient for the customers rather than for you.

Tips for Service Businesses

- Show up on time and be polite and respectful.
- Try to do a little bit more than the customer expects.
- Ask each customer if there's anything special you should know before you start the job.
- Dress appropriately for your work conditions.
- Clean up after you are done.
- Keep a calendar to schedule your future jobs.

PRODUCT BUSINESSES

To begin a product business, you need to find something that customers are willing to buy.

Tips for Product Businesses

- Buy good-quality materials.
- Schedule your time well so you'll be sure to *finish* the craft projects that you start.
- Plan carefully, and sketch your designs and ideas on paper first.
- Budget your expenses, so you don't spend more than you can earn by selling your product.

You can either make your product yourself or buy things and re-sell them. An advantage of a product business is that you can do much of the work whenever you want. On the other hand, you will have to buy or make your product before you can sell it, so it can cost more money and take more time to get started.

How to pick a business

It depends entirely on you. Running a business means putting in a lot of work. Of course, it's only "work" if you don't like doing it. So ask yourself these questions before you decide on a business:

WHAT DO YOU LIKE DOING?

Do you have any hobbies or interests that you'd like to pursue? Many businesses have been started by people who just wanted to spend more time on their hobbies. If you choose something you like to do, then it will be a lot easier to spend your time doing it.

WHAT ARE YOU GOOD AT?

You might have a skill that can be turned into a business. Are you artistically talented? Are you great with computers? If you have a special talent, there could be many ways to take advantage of it. And the more you do it, the better you'll get!

 WHAT DO PEOPLE NEED OR WANT?

Take a good look around. You might be the first one to notice a need for a product or service that other people will pay for. Did you know that earmuffs were invented by a kid? He certainly wasn't the first person to get cold ears, but he was the first one to come up with a good way to solve the problem!

Spend some time thinking about these questions. They should help give you some ideas for your business. Later we will look at some business ideas that other kids have already done—thirty of them! To get an idea of what type of business might be right for you, try the following quiz.

The story of earmuffs

Chester Greenwood was fifteen years old in 1873. He and the other kids in Farmington, Maine, loved to spend time sledding and ice skating, but the winters were so frosty that Chester's ears would get painfully cold. He finally decided to solve the problem himself by creating a device that held warm fabric against his ears. He called them "ear muffs" and started selling them. They became so popular that within a few years he owned a factory and sold them all across the country. Chester ran this business and others for the rest of his life.

The questions in this quiz are designed to help you decide which business might be best for you. The Thirty Great Business Ideas in Part 2 of this book are organized into sections based on the questions below. There will probably be more than one kind of activity that matches your skills and interests. So here we go . . .

1. *Do you like talking to people, even people who you just met?*
Consider businesses that involve selling things, teaching, and entertaining.

2. *Do you like making things with your hands?*
Look at crafts, such as making jewelry and building birdhouses.

3. *Do you like being outside?*
Look into businesses with an outdoor focus, such as washing cars or doing yard work.

4. *Do you like to paint or draw?*
Consider an artistic business such as face painting or making greeting cards.

5. *Do you like using your computer?*
Consider activities such as word processing, desktop publishing, or being a computer consultant.

6. *Do you like being around animals?*
Take a look at businesses such as pet-sitting, cage cleaning, and dog walking.

You may find that more than one category applies to you. That's okay! It means you have more options from which to choose. Now that you have an idea of the kind of business that's right for you, let's look at your skills.

SKILLS

Skills are an important part of any successful business. For instance, it would be hard to make much money juggling if you didn't know how to juggle!

There are two ways that you can get the skills you need for a job. The first way is to be born with a talent—that's the lucky way. The normal way, however, is to learn a skill and practice until you've mastered it.

How to get the right skills

If you want to learn a new skill or improve one that you already have, the first thing to do is to learn more about it. Find a friend or a relative who already knows how to make jewelry, or wash a car, or build a birdhouse (or whatever else you want to learn), and ask him or her to teach you. If possible, check out how your competitors do it. Borrow books or videos from the library. Take a class. Join a club. Then practice, practice, and practice some more!

Do you want to run a lawn-mowing business? Offer to mow your family's lawn for practice. Do you want to be a face painter? Ask your friends to let you paint their faces, or paint your little brother's face while he's asleep. (Just kidding!) Do you want to make and sell bird feeders? Make one for your own backyard and see if the birds like it. If not, try another design.

What's the worst that can happen?

For many people, the hardest part of a business is talking to new people. It's perfectly normal to be shy. Here are some hints on how to get past it:

- Smile! If you look friendly, your customers will start talking to you first.

- Show your customers a sample product or pictures of your work. It can be much easier to talk to people if they're looking at something other than you!

- Ask your customers friendly questions such as "Are you keeping cool during this heat wave?" or "That's a cute dog—what kind is it?" The more you think about the people you're talking to, the less you'll worry about yourself.

Doing a good job

Whatever type of business you do, it's important that you do it well. When people pay you, they expect you to do a good job. If the customers aren't happy, then they won't come back. And they won't send their friends to you, either! On the other hand, if you do the best kids' parties in town (or word processing, or window cleaning, or whatever) you'll have more business than you can handle. The other nice thing about improving your skills is that you can often finish your work faster. And if you do it faster, you can fit more jobs in, and earn more money!

TOOLS AND MATERIALS

After deciding which business you are going to pursue, part of your research will be to find out exactly what tools and materials you need to get started. Depending on what kind of job you have chosen, this could be just a few simple items (leaf raking doesn't take much!) or quite a bit of stuff (like running a lemonade-plus stand).

Borrowing tools

See if someone you know will let you borrow his or her tools when you get started. (Maybe you can offer them services or products from your business as "rental payment" for the equipment.) If your business starts to take off, though, you'll want to buy your own tools. You don't want the owner to come and take back his tools while you're right in the middle of using them.

Buying tools and materials

When you buy tools, figure out how much you can spend, then get the best you can afford. For instance, if you do a lot of weeding, you'll find that a better-quality hand trowel will last a lot longer than a "bargain" one. Better tools will allow you to do your job more easily and quickly.

The same is true for the materials you use. If you make jewelry with poor-quality plastic beads, your customers won't be very impressed. People want the services they pay for and the things they buy to be high quality. Your goal is to make the customer happy.

That doesn't mean that you shouldn't buy carefully. Even if you are looking for good-quality materials and tools, you can often save a lot of money by shopping around. Look for your tools in warehouse stores or superstores. Buy materials in bulk if you can. The more money you save, the easier it

will be to make a profit (more on that later).

Try to choose tools and materials that will not harm the environment, such as biodegradable soaps, nontoxic cleaners, recycled or recyclable materials, lawn mowers that are pushed rather than gasoline-powered, and so on. You'll be doing a good turn for the environment, and your customers will appreciate it, too!

Taking care of your tools

Once you have your tools, take good care of them. Cleaning up may not be much fun, but remember, if you don't take care of your tools, they will get ruined. Then you will have to spend more money (ouch!) to buy new ones.

SAFETY

Many of the tools and materials that you will use can, if misused, hurt you and others. Always carefully read the directions for everything you use in your business. Always ask an adult for help if you are at all unsure about the proper, safe use of your tools and materials. Do not take risks with your safety—it's not worth it!

CUSTOMERS

This may seem really obvious, but you can't have a business without customers. (Well, I suppose you could, but you can't have a *successful* business without customers!)

Who is your target market?

Different businesses have different customers. For instance, some products might appeal to young kids (puppets), while some might appeal to older kids or adults (key chains). Part of running a business is finding out just who your customers are going to be—they are called your *target market*. Knowing who makes up your target market will help you focus your products and services, set your prices, and choose where and when to advertise.

Taking your business to the customer

It's important to set up your business where you can best reach your target customers. Sometimes it helps to set up a table, like a lemonade stand. Choose the location of your table carefully. For instance, you could probably sell a lot of lemonade at a Little League baseball park on a hot day.

If you decide to make and sell crafts, look into selling them at school, or setting up a table at a fair or holiday bazaar. These are special events run by churches, schools, and other organizations. It usually costs money to rent a table, so you will have to make enough sales to pay the fee. Ask at your local craft store to find out when and where some of these events might be.

Communicating with your customer

Talk to your customers! It's always important to establish good communication, and this is especially true for a service business. Before you start the job, make sure that your responsibilities are clear—and theirs, too. It's a lot easier to correct a misunderstand-

Andrew's Lemonade Stand

I had my first business experience when I was eight years old. I needed some money to buy cool stuff. And what better way to make some quick cash than with a lemonade stand?

I made a big "Lemonade, 10 cents!" sign and plastered it to a table in front of my house. As I was fixing up my stand, my friend Kim came over and wanted to help out. I told her that I would give her fifty cents and all the lemonade she wanted if she helped me get customers. She agreed and quickly went to work. However, we just weren't getting many people to stop.

Finally, I realized it was because the drivers going past didn't know about the lemonade until it was too late to stop. The next day, we made a huge sign for the stand, with bright colors and big letters so everyone could easily read it. Then we picked up shop and moved down the block to a four-way stop intersection. Since the cars had to stop at the stop sign anyway, there was no excuse for them to pass up some great lemonade. They would just roll down their window and buy a glass of lemonade—it was very simple. Soon enough, the money started pouring in!

For the rest of the summer, we set up the stand every day at the corner. It was a great success: I had a great time, made a large sum of spending money, and learned some valuable lessons about business and how it works.

Andrew Zupnick, age 19

ing *before* it happens. You wouldn't want to pull up someone's favorite flowers while weeding their garden, for example. You should also ask your customers if they have a preference for the products you use—whether it's a favorite doggy treat or a better car wax. Many businesses are successful because they listen to their customers!

There are many times, especially with service businesses, when it is a good idea to have a contract with your customers. A contract clearly states what the service is that you are going to provide for the customer, when you will provide it, and how much the customer will pay when you are done.

Although contracts aren't legal documents until you are an adult, a contract can still help to prevent misunderstandings and hard feelings. See page 103 for information on how to create a contract.

Selling your product on consignment

If you don't want to set up a booth, you can try to sell items on *consignment.* This means that you find a store that will try to sell your things for you. You don't get paid until your products are sold, and then you split the money with the store. Many stores that sell arts and crafts are run this way.

If you are interested, talk to the manager of a store that sells the kinds of things that you want to make. Find out if the store handles consignments and how much money (what percentage) they take from the sale. Have your parents check over the details of any contracts, though!

Advertise!

If you want the customers to come to you, then it's time to start advertising. The KidBiz Disk has files to help you prepare business cards, flyers, and print advertisements. (See page 98 for more information on how to make these for your business.) What are each of these things?

- *Business cards* are small, wallet-size cards that you give to current and potential customers so they can have your business name and contact information handy.

- *Flyers* are half-size or full-size sheets of paper with eye-catching designs and more detailed information about your business. Post your flyers or hand them out in places where your potential customers are. Or ask your current customers to pass your flyers on to their friends.

- *Print advertisements* are notices with information about your business that your school or local newspaper or newsletter can print, for a fee.

Here are some things to think about when you make your advertising materials:

✓ Choose a good name for your business. Try to make it something that people will remember.

✓ Try to make up a catchy slogan: "Dawn's Lawns: You grow it, we mow it!"

✓ Describe your product or service clearly. But keep it short!

✓ Include the phone number or address of your business, and your E-mail address, if you have one.

✓ Check carefully for errors in spelling or grammar. (You wouldn't believe how many adults who run businesses make this mistake!)

Get your advertising out there

Once you've made your advertising materials, you have to get them in the right places. The easiest thing to do is to go through your neighborhood and leave flyers under every door or in every paper box. (Don't put them in mailboxes, though. They're reserved for U.S. mail.) You can also give them to your friends, or hand them out at school. You can post flyers on bulletin boards in many places—churches, synagogues, schools, senior centers, community centers, and more. Try to put your flyers in places that your target customers might visit. (Think of it as fishing. Put your bait where the fish are!)

FOR INSTANCE,

- If your business is pet care, see if you can put up signs at the pet store and a veterinarian's office.
- If you do yard care, post flyers at the local nursery or garden center.
- If you make crafts, post your flyers at a craft store.

Introduce yourself to the managers at the businesses where you want to post flyers. Ask if there is a place where you can put your flyers, like a window or a bulletin board. Even if you can't put up a sign, leave a couple of your business cards with the manager or an employee. They may send customers your way!

Once your business is up and running, give some of your flyers and business cards to your customers and ask them to mention you to their friends. Many successful businesses find their customers through word of mouth.

There are many creative ways to market your work. You can:

- Leave a sign in the garden that you weed: "This garden weeded by No Weeds, Indeed. Call 555-WEED for info."

- Wear a T-shirt with your business name when you mow lawns, wash windows, or do other outdoor jobs.

- If you're a computer consultant, tape your business card to your customers' computers. This gives them an easy place to find your phone number in an emergency, and it's free advertising for you!

- If you make puppets or other crafts, attach tags to your handiwork with the name of your company and how to contact you.

WHAT OTHER WAYS CAN YOU THINK OF TO MARKET YOUR BUSINESS?

Keeping customers

After you have found your customers, the next step is just as important—*keeping* your customers. One of the most important rules for keeping a business going is to always be nice to your customers. (Even when it's your little brother.) People are much more likely to hire you or buy things from you if they like you. Happy customers will come back again, and they will tell their friends about you, too.

On the other hand, if a customer leaves unhappy, they probably won't come back—and they'll tell their friends about that, too! So, if there is something wrong with your product or service, either replace it, redo it, or give the customer their money back. For instance, if there's a bug in their lemonade, give them another cup of lemonade for free. And do it with a smile!

Making a good impression

Some other ways to make good impressions on your customers are:

BE POLITE AND SMILE.

• Always do a little more than the customer expects. For example, add a free mint to their order. Or bring a doggy treat when you come to walk their dog.

• Offer special **DEALS** for repeat customers: "Buy four necklaces, get one free!"

BE NEAT AND CLEAN

• If you sell from a booth, take the time to decorate the booth and make it look nice. Don't let it get too messy.

• If you are sending mail or notices to your customers, use the files from the KidBiz Disk to make professional-looking stationery.

How much should you charge?

The answer to that question is—it depends! Choosing your prices is a balancing act. You want to make enough money to pay all your expenses and have some left over. You also want your prices to look like a good deal for your customers.

Competition

If someone else is trying to sell similar products or services as yours, then you have *competition*. The best way to respond to competition is to find out more about it! Check out how they run their business, how much they charge, and how good a job they do. After you know all about them, you may discover some new ways to improve *your* own business. You can make your product or service better, set your prices lower, choose a slightly different target market—or do all of these things!

If you sell products, you need to look at how much it takes to buy your materials, and how long it takes you to make and sell your items. If you have a service, you can charge by the hour, or by the job. Make sure your price covers the cost of the tools and materials that you need to buy.

A good way to check your prices is to look at other businesses like yours. Check what their prices are and see if you can run your business at those prices—or maybe even a little bit less. But be careful not to charge too low a price. You'll soon lose interest in a business that earns you only a few cents an hour!

If you have ever gone on a long car trip with your family, your parents probably had maps and directions, and most importantly, they knew where you were all going!

You need the same kinds of information when you get ready to start your business. You need to figure out what you are going to do, how you are going to do it, and when you are going to do it. Start thinking about the questions in the questionnaire on the next page. (Did you think that running your own business meant that you wouldn't have homework? I hate to break it to you, but businesspeople have homework, too!) After you choose a business idea, write down your answers to these questions. This is your *business plan*.

But don't worry! Even if you already have an idea for your business, you almost certainly won't know all the answers yet. That's okay. You're not supposed to. The questions are here to help guide your research as you make your plan.

The business plan questionnaire

1. What is the name of your business? Think of something catchy that customers will remember and that also makes it clear what your business does or sells.

2. What is your product or service?

3. What skills will you need? How will you learn these skills?

4. What tools and materials will it take to get started?

5. How much time will it take to get started?

6. How much money will it take to get started? Figure out what your tools and materials will cost you. Are there any other costs?

7. How much time can you spend on your business each week?

8. Who will need your product or service? Who are most likely to be your customers? Neighbors? Classmates? Pet owners? This is your target market.

9. How will you advertise your business? Try to focus your advertising in places where your target customers will see it.

10. How much time and money will you spend on advertising?

11. How much do other people charge for a similar service or product? Ask around. Learn about your competition.

12. How much are you going to charge? The trick is to set your prices low enough that people will want to pay, but high enough that you can have money left after paying expenses.

Setting goals

Once you have a business plan, you need to set goals. These will help you measure your progress. Some examples might be:

• My business will be ready to open by May 1, in time for Little League season.

• I will have six lawn-mowing customers signed up by June 15.

• I will sell fifty glasses of lemonade a week by August 1.

Use your goals to keep your plan on track. Don't set your goals too high, though. That can be frustrating. Instead, choose a realistic goal that you think you can achieve in a short period of time. This is called a short-term goal. If you meet that goal, celebrate and reward yourself! Then immediately set another one. If you miss a goal, adjust your plan or revise your goals, and give it another try. It's good to have a long-term goal in mind, but it's most important that you have realistic short-term goals as well.

Michael's Crafts

One day, Nina, Jessica, Scott, Alyia, and I made lanyard, cards, necklaces, and bracelets to sell. It was a hot day, and we were sweating. It is hard starting your own business. You have to have the right attitude. You have to have patience because sometimes the customers do not come quickly. You have to have a business plan, you have to know the cost of everything, and you have to be a fast thinker.

Michael Chatman, Jr., age 10

Making a budget

Many of the questions in the business plan questionnaire deal with how much money you make, which is called *revenue*, and how much you spend, which is called *expenses*. One of the hard parts of running a business is making sure that you have more revenue than expenses. You can do this by creating a *budget*. A budget is your

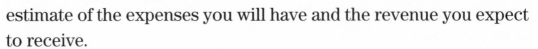

estimate of the expenses you will have and the revenue you expect to receive.

If your revenue is higher than your expenses, then you will have money left over. This is called a *profit*. If your expenses are more than your revenue, then you will lose money. This is called a *loss*. It is important to plan ahead to be sure your business will make a profit, rather than a loss.

The good news is that you can use a special program on the KidBiz disk called a *spreadsheet* to help you do this. (See page 89 for instructions on using the KidBiz spreadsheet.) What is a spreadsheet? It is a computer program that helps you keep track of your revenue and expenses. It even calculates your profit for you. Before you start your business you can enter your estimated revenue and expenses into the spreadsheet, then do something called "what if."

• What if your sales are a little lower than you expect?

• What if your costs go up a bit? Would you still make a profit?

Change the numbers in your spreadsheet and see! By trying out different estimated amounts of revenue and expenses, you can do a better job of planning your business.

Adjusting revenue and expenses

Once you start your business, you can make a new spreadsheet to help track your actual revenue and expenses. Compare how much they are with how much you expected they would be in your estimate. Did you make a profit?

If you take a loss, don't panic! That just means that it's time to rework your business plan. Take another look at the business plan questionnaire and look for ways to increase your revenue or reduce your expenses. Try out some new numbers in your spreadsheet.

The Bottom Line

You might have heard people talk about the "bottom line." This is originally a business phrase, of course. Companies used to use special books to write down their revenue and expenses. They subtracted the expenses from the revenue, and on the bottom line—the last line on the paper—they wrote down the figures that showed whether the company was earning or losing money.

Today, the term "bottom line" means the end result, or the final profit or loss.

HOW TO INCREASE REVENUE

✔ Advertise more, or in different places.

✔ Try a different sales location where there may be more people who are likely to buy your product or service.

✔ Lower your prices if you think people are not buying your product or service because they find it too expensive.

✔ Or, raise your prices if you think customers will pay more. But be careful—you don't want your loyal customers to be unhappy.

HOW TO REDUCE EXPENSES

✔ Buy less expensive supplies.

✔ Eliminate items you are trying to sell that aren't very popular. Or try to find a way to improve them.

✔ Reduce your advertising costs. Ask your customers how they found you. If your paid advertising isn't working, then it's not worth the expense.

✔ Try to get more business through personal recommendations.

Funding your business

There's an old saying—"It takes money to make money." And it's true! For almost any business that you start, you will have expenses *before* you have revenue. After you figure out how much money it will take to start up your business, you have to figure out where to get that money. Here are some ideas:

- Save your allowance. This shouldn't be too hard if your starting expenses are low.

- Get a loan from your parents. You could agree to a schedule for paying the money back based on your business plan.

- Earn extra money doing odd jobs around the house or jobs with low start-up costs, such as baby-sitting. Once you have enough saved, you can start the business you really want.

That's enough background to get started. Now it's time to decide what your business is going to be. Each of the Thirty Great Business Ideas that follow will list some hints to help you put your plan together. You will also find listings of books and other resource materials at the back of the book. Take a look through them and see which ones sound good to you!

PART 2

THIRTY GREAT BUSINESS IDEAS!

The business ideas on the following pages range from tried-and-true favorites such as lawn mowing to more unusual businesses such as selling handmade greeting cards.

You may want to adapt these ideas to work best for you. Some might not be right for you at all. Use these examples to start thinking about your *own* ideas for businesses.

OUTDOOR ✿ ✿ ✿ BUSINESSES

1. LAWN MOWING

Establish yourself as someone who can do a good job of cutting grass, and you should be able to keep quite busy—because it all grows back!

SKILLS

You should be able to:

- Safely operate a lawn mower and grass clippers.
- Cut a lawn and edge it neatly.
- Rake and clean up afterward.

TOOLS AND MATERIALS

You will need:

- A lawn mower (Electric or hand-powered mowers don't require messing with gasoline, so they might be a good choice for a small job).
- Grass clippers for edging.

- Extension cord (if you use anything electric).
- Gasoline can and gas (if you are using a gas mower).
- Rake.

- Garden gloves.
- Safety glasses if there are sticks, rocks, or other debris on the lawn.
- Large garbage bags.

HELPFUL HINTS

- Lawn mowers can be very dangerous. Before you do this job, work with an adult to understand exactly how to use one safely.
- Try to schedule your lawn cutting during the cooler part of the day.
- Use the grass clippers for neatening the edges of the yard. Be thorough!
- Clean up after you're done. This includes bagging the grass clippings and putting tools away.
- Work as quickly and efficiently as you can. No one wants to pay you for taking a break in the shade!
- Offer to weed your customer's garden—for an additional fee, of course.

CUSTOMERS

- Ask your customers to let you put a small sign in the corner of their yard that says YARD MOWED BY DAWN'S LAWNS. (Using your business name, of course!)

When does a job become a business?

You've probably already done work for other people, such as yard work, baby-sitting, or taking in someone's mail. When do jobs like this become a business?

When they take planning! Doing an occasional odd job doesn't take much planning, but if you start working more, then it helps to get organized. This includes scheduling your time, budgeting, advertising, and all the other things described in this book. It requires more work than odd jobs—but you'll probably earn more money!

- Talk to managers of office parks or stores that have yards. These jobs can be much bigger and pay a lot more than your neighbor's lawn.

2. LEAF RAKING

In many parts of the country, fall is a time when the leaves drop from the trees and cover everyone's yard. Somebody has to clean them up—and it might as well be you!

SKILLS

You should be able to:

- Rake and clean up leaves from the yard and garden and bag them.
- Pay attention to details and have the patience to do a thorough job.

TOOLS AND MATERIALS

You will need:

- A rake.
- Garden gloves.
- Yard bags to hold the leaves.
- A large plastic garbage can.
- A small hand rake.

HELPFUL HINTS

- Wear gloves to prevent blisters.
- Use a small hand rake—or your hands—to get leaves out from under shrubs or between smaller plants.
- Bagging leaves is easier if you put the yard bag into a large trash can to hold it open.
- Ask your customer if there's a wooded area on the property where you can deposit the leaves, to save the trouble of bagging them.

CUSTOMERS

- Since the leaves will keep falling for a while, try to sign your customers up for regular weekly visits.
- Take before-and-after pictures and show them to potential customers, or post them with your flyers.
- A good place to advertise is at your local nursery.
- If you live in an area that gets a lot of snow, try to sign up your customers ahead of time for snow shoveling.

3. SNOW SHOVELING

Snow is anything but fun for many adults. They would probably be more than happy to pay you to shovel it for them.

SKILLS

You should be able to:

- Work hard! It's not easy shoveling heavy snow.
- Do a thorough job so there are no slick spots.
- Work outside in very cold weather (bundle up!).
- Get up early in the morning on snowy days, so your customers can get to work on time.

TOOLS AND MATERIALS

You will need:

- A good, sturdy snow shovel.
- A nice warm coat, scarf, hat, and gloves.
- Waterproof boots. (It would be a shame to waste your earnings on doctor bills for frostbite.)
- A bag of sand.

HELPFUL HINTS

■ Buy your shovel in the fall before the first snow, because they can disappear in a hurry when the snow hits!

■ Practice shoveling your own driveway and walk to see how well you can do it and how long it takes. (I'm sure your parents would be more than happy to have you do it, too!)

■ You may want to bring a bag of sand and sprinkle it on the shoveled walks to keep them from getting slippery. Check with the owners first, however.

CUSTOMERS

■ Decide at the beginning of the winter how many homes you think you can handle, and try to sign up your customers ahead of time.

■ Find a snapshot of a previous snowstorm and take it with you when you approach potential customers. It will help them remember what a pain it was to clear their driveway themselves! Or show *before* and *after* photos of a driveway you've shoveled.

4. CAR WASHING

People really like their cars to be shiny and clean. Sounds like a paying job for a kid.

SKILLS

You should be able to:

■ Pay attention to detail.

■ Work quickly.

TOOLS AND MATERIALS

You will need:

■ A large sponge for washing.

■ Soft rags, for polishing and drying.

■ A bucket.

■ Mild dishwashing soap (NOT the stuff for the dishwasher!).

- A scrub brush for hubcaps.
- A small brush (like an old tooth-brush) for details.
- A step stool and a sponge with a handle for the roof—especially for larger vehicles.
- Access to a hose or other water source.
- A hand-held vacuum cleaner for the interior.
- Liquid car wax.

HELPFUL HINTS

- Use a brush to get all the dirt from around the headlights, the grille, and the hubcaps.
- If the weather is chilly, fill your soap bucket with warm water—your fingers will thank you! (Warm water cleans better, too.)
- Don't wear clothes with metal buttons and zippers. As you lean across the car to wash it, these can scratch the paint. That's not a good way to get repeat customers!
- Make sure to use lots of soapy water when you're cleaning, otherwise the little bits of dirt can scratch the paint on the car.

- If someone you know has a nice car that they wash a lot, volunteer to help them and watch how they do it.
- Ask your customer if they have any special cleaning or waxing products that they would like you to use. (Some people are very particular about their cars!)

CUSTOMERS

- Wash the family car and put a sign on it when it's parked in front of your house.
- Leave your business card in the corner of the window of the cars you wash.
- If you live near water, expand your business to washing boats too.

5. WINDOW CLEANING

Window washing is one of those jobs adults really dislike, so it's a good opportunity for you!

SKILLS

You should be able to:

■ Get a window clean and streak-free. Practice on the windows in your house until you can get perfectly clean windows every time. (You'll get faster, too!)

TOOLS AND MATERIALS

You will need:

■ A bucket.
■ Glass-cleaning liquid, such as Windex.
■ Some clean, dry rags.
■ A squeegee—the kind with a rubber edge on one side and a sponge on the other.

HELPFUL HINTS

■ Use a squeegee with a long handle to avoid having to climb on ladders to reach the tops of tall windows. Keep your feet on the ground!

- How much you charge depends on the size, kind, and number of windows that you wash. After you've had some practice, you should be able to look at windows and have a good idea of how long it will take to clean them.

- Use a squeegee to "scrape" the soapy water from the glass, and then use a rag to dry the edge of the squeegee after every stroke. It leaves nice streak-free windows!

- For this job, details really count! Make sure that you completely clean up after yourself, don't leave puddles, and of course, leave clean windows.

CUSTOMERS

- Wear a T-shirt advertising your business while you wash, or put a sign out in the yard while you work that says something like WILLIAM'S WINDOW WASHING.

Melissa's Cleaning Service

I was interested in earning money, so one day I said to my mom, "Mom, I'm going to do chores for two dollars a day, a dollar for each thing I do." I washed dishes and did a lot of sweeping.

My mom had me doing so much work I was exhausted. Then she told more people about the good work I do and they wanted me to do all their work. I vacuumed, mopped, washed dishes, and cleaned the tub. I wanted to faint, but when I was finished I saw how much money I had made. I made seven dollars at each house. Including mine, I made ninety-eight dollars. I saved it up and my mom was happy. What a business.

Melissa Harris, age 9

ANIMAL ★ ★ ★ BUSINESSES

6. CAGE CLEANING

Many people keep pets. Animals make wonderful friends, but they can also make an amazing mess. Someone needs to clean it up—how about you?

SKILLS

You should be able to:

- Get along with animals.
- Feel comfortable about cleaning up messes—sometimes really stinky ones!

TOOLS AND MATERIALS

You will need:

- Rubber gloves.
- A bucket.
- Mild liquid dishwashing soap (not the kind for the dishwasher).
- Scrub brush, old toothbrush, sponges, clean rags.
- Old newspapers to line the cage.

HELPFUL HINTS

- Check with your local pet store or veterinarian for advice on how to clean cages.
- Pay attention to detail. Every corner needs to be washed and rinsed thoroughly to make sure that the cage is a safe and healthy place.
- Ask your customer to provide a safe place for the pet to be while you clean its cage.

CUSTOMERS

- Pet shops and veterinarians' offices are good places to advertise. They can also connect you to organizations that might be helpful, such as clubs for owners of reptiles, birds, or other critters.

7. DOG WALKING

Sometimes life gets very busy for people. They'll probably be glad to get help walking the dog.

SKILLS

You should be able to:

- Be comfortable around dogs.
- Be strong enough to walk a large dog.
- Be responsible! Your customers' pets are very important to them.

TOOLS AND MATERIALS

You will need:

- Comfortable walking shoes, because walking is what this job is all about.
- A pooper-scooper.
- Some plastic bags for the you-know-what! Scooping dogs' poop is not only the polite thing to do, in some places it's also the law.

HELPFUL HINTS

- Keep your four-footed friends happy and reward them for good behavior with doggy treats. If you bring treats every time you walk the dog, you'll become one of its very best friends! (Make sure it's okay with the owner first.)
- Ask each dog owner if there's anything in particular you should know about the dog (if he barks at small children, chases cars, etc.).
- You might want to buy a can of dog-repelling spray. Even though *your* dog is leashed, some other people let their dogs run loose. Use it only as a last resort to drive away a dog that is getting too aggressive with your dog. Ask your pet store or veterinarian for their recommendation for a product.
- If you can handle several dogs, arrange to walk up to four dogs at once. You'll save time and make more money.

CUSTOMERS

- Put up signs in pet stores and veterinarians' offices.
- Wear a T-shirt with the name and number of your business when you're walking a dog.

8. DOG GROOMING

Dogs can get really dirty. Why not offer to wash them?

SKILLS

You should be able to:

- Be comfortable around animals.
- Learn how to take a dog through the washing process, and learn good brushing techniques. It'll be a little different for, say, a Chihuahua than for an English sheepdog!

TOOLS AND MATERIALS

You will need:

- Appropriate shampoo and brushes (ask the owner if they have a preference for what you should use).
- Rubber gloves.
- Clean, dry towels.

HELPFUL HINTS

- Charge separately for washing and brushing. Many dogs don't need to be washed every week, but many need a good brushing at least once a week (especially during shedding season).

- Have the owners prepare a place where you can wash the dog at their house. If the weather is nice, you can do the job out in the yard with the hose. If not, you may need to wash the dog in the bathtub.

- As soon as you're done with the final rinse, get a towel over the dog right away. (If you don't, he'll shake the water off and give *you* a bath.)

- Talk to the dog gently while you work, and give it lots of praise for being cooperative.

- This job can be pretty messy. Always take the time to clean up water and dog hair after you're done.

- One last trick: If it's okay with the owner, bring a supply of doggy treats with you. Give the dog one when you first arrive, when you finish each step of the job (washing, drying, brushing), and just before you leave. That way the dog will learn to really like you—and he will be more cooperative, too.

CUSTOMERS

- Advertise in local pet stores and veterinarians' offices.

Aaron's Pet-Sitting

To make money I baby-sat my friend's pets while he and his family went on vacation. I love nature, so I had fun doing it, and picked up some extra money, too! He gave me the food and directions to take good care of his frog and two gerbils.

The week was over in what felt like two seconds. The job was great, and so was the payment. I recommend this job to anyone who likes nature and likes to play with animals.

Aaron Kaplan Bradley, age 10

- Take *before* and *after* pictures to show potential customers and to put in your advertisements.

- Call your customers a few weeks after your visit to remind them to schedule their dog's next bath.

9. PET-SITTING AND HOUSE WATCHING

Many people care a lot about their pets. So when they go on vacation, they want to know that their beloved companions are well taken care of. People without pets may also want to have their house looked after while they're on vacation. You could be just the person for the job!

SKILLS

You should be able to:

- Feel comfortable around animals.
- Be very dependable and trustworthy. Your customers would not be very happy if you forgot to feed their goldfish while they were away!

TOOLS AND MATERIALS

You will need:

- A notepad to record specific chores and other information.
  - A safe place to keep the house keys.

HELPFUL HINTS

- Be careful. If you can, bring a parent or older brother or sister along when you visit the house. *Never go into a house that looks like it has been broken into!*
- Visit the home before the vacationers leave to meet the animals and go over the details—how much to feed the pets, when to water the plants, where to put the mail, what lights to turn on when, and so on.
- Be sure to ask if there's an alarm system for the house, and how to turn it off and back on. Write it all down!
- Make yourself a schedule and checklist.
- Make sure that you have emergency phone numbers, the number where

the owners will be, and the name and number of their neighbor or veterinarian in case something happens.

- Be careful to leave the house exactly as you found it after each visit—turn off the lights (unless the owners left them on intentionally), lock the doors, and clean up after yourself and the animals.

- If anything unusual happens (like a blackout, or a branch falls on their patio) leave the owners a note giving any important details. Actually, it's a good idea to leave a note saying that everything went fine, too.

CUSTOMERS

- Find customers from among your neighbors and family friends.

- Do not go to meet with a potential customer without your parents' permission. Never go to the home of someone you don't know!

- Ask customers to write you a letter of reference when you have completed a job. Show it to potential new customers to convince them that you are trustworthy.

Elizabeth's Kittens

"Meow, meow." Boy, were Victoria and Minerva hungry! I was across the street taking care of my neighbor's two six-week-old kittens. That was my job for part of the summer. I had to feed them, give them water, play with them, change their litter box—everything!

Every morning, after I got up and got dressed, I took care of them. They were babies, and they needed love. It was so much fun. At the end of two long weeks, I got paid forty dollars. You don't know how proud I was. I would have done it for free, because they were so cute, but I enjoyed getting the money.

Elizabeth Zagar, age 10

- Ask customers if you can use pictures of their pets in your advertising.

PEOPLE BUSINESSES

10. GIFT WRAPPING

Holidays add extra stress to adults' lives. Help them enjoy those special times of the year by wrapping their presents for them!

SKILLS

You should be able to:

- Neatly wrap a package and tie a ribbon. Practice until your corners and edges look professional.
- Learn how to do really spiffy wrapping jobs. If you can, find someone who can show you how to do tricks, like ribbons with fancy curls.
- Keep the packages organized so you can remember which ones belong to which person!

TOOLS AND MATERIALS

You will need:

- A variety of wrapping papers, ribbons, boxes, and gift tags (buy them in bulk at warehouse stores to save money).
- Good scissors.
- Glue (for adding special decorations).
- Tape.
- A flat, clean work space where you can spread out.
- Cards and labels to attach to each package.

HELPFUL HINTS

- To really add pizzazz to your wrapping, look for small decorations to add to your packages. (Check out your local craft, fabric, or party supply stores for ideas that don't cost very much.) Even little pinecones attached to the ribbon can add a nice touch. Be creative!

- Use glue or tape to attach the decorations firmly so that they don't fall off.

CUSTOMERS

- Display several examples of the kinds of wrapping you can do (with empty packages, of course!) to show potential customers.
- Put up flyers before major holidays at school and on bulletin boards of local churches, synagogues, and senior centers.

- Get permission to set up a table at school or in busy shopping areas.
- Try to run this business from your home if you can. There's a lot of competition in the mall from fund-raising programs and free store gift-wrapping.

Read On!

Hauser, Priscilla. *Create Your Own Greeting Cards & Gift Wrap*. Cincinnati, Ohio: North Light Books, 1994.

11. CHILDREN'S PARTIES

If you'd like to be a party organizer, then you can have fun twice—running the party, and then getting paid for it!

SKILLS

You should be able to:

- Enjoy being around younger kids.
- Be friendly, energetic, and very, very patient. (Kids at parties tend to be just a little bit excited!)
- Be organized and be able to plan out details.
- Know how to set up and run exciting activities, games, and other fun things to keep little kids entertained.

TOOLS AND MATERIALS

You will need:

- Party favors and goody bags.
- Decorations.
- Paper plates, cups, plastic forks and spoons.
- Snacks, drinks, cake, and ice cream.
- Equipment for games and activities.
- A portable stereo and tapes or CDs (if you are providing music).

HELPFUL HINTS

- Find out how many kids are expected and how old they are.
- Find out well in advance what your customer expects you to do. Are you just in charge of the entertainment? What about snacks? Decorations? Party favors? Cleanup? It's a good idea to have your customer sign a contract (like the one on the KidBiz Disk) describing your responsibilities—and theirs, too.
- Make yourself a checklist to use when you meet with the customer to decide on what kind of cake and ice cream to have, and what kinds of games and activities to prepare. Suggest a theme for the party— sports, cartoons, ballet, or whatever other ideas you can think of.
- To really get the kids' attention and add a little zest to the party, dress up to match the theme of the party.

- If you have a special talent, such as playing the guitar, face painting, or putting on a great puppet show, be sure to mention it to your customer.
- Do all the cleanup after the party for the parents.
- Charge your customer according to the number of children expected at the party.

CUSTOMERS

- Post your flyers at local party supply stores, toy stores, day care centers, and preschools.
- Put small stickers with your business's name and phone number on the bottom of the goody bags that the guests take home.

12. GARAGE SALE MANAGER

Everyone loves to get rid of old things with a garage sale, but many don't like the hassle of setting it up. You can offer to help out and run it for them for a little bit of the profit.

SKILLS

You should be able to:

- Be very organized.
- Handle money and make change accurately and quickly.
- Keep a record of everything that sells.
- Plan ahead.

TOOLS AND MATERIALS

You will need:

- Tables.
- Chairs.
- Colored sticky dots to use as price tags.
- A record book to record sales.
- Receipts.
- Change for people making purchases.
- A yard or garage to set up stuff.
- A backup plan if you set up outdoors and it begins to rain!
- Signs, and strong waterproof tape for hanging them.
- A calculator.

HELPFUL HINTS

- Plan to spend at least two weeks putting this together. Have everything sorted and priced by the night before the sale.
- Discuss your fee with the customer beforehand. You can charge a fixed amount or a percentage of the profits.
- Put signs on each table labeling the category of items on that table (kitchen, artwork, books, etc.).
- If you're selling clothes, try to get a rack to hang them on.
- Consider setting up a lemonade and snack stand, too.

- You can run one big yard sale for several families at once. Give each family a different color of sticky dots to put on their stuff. The dots will be price tags, and will also help you keep track of who the merchandise belonged to. Keep a notebook with different pages for each family, to record each item you sell and how much you sell it for.

- If the project gets really big, ask your friends to help out in exchange for a share of the profits.

CUSTOMERS

- Put ads in the classified section of your local and school newspapers

the weekend of the sale, and put signs around the neighborhood the day before the sale. Note the date, hours, and location of the sale. Write with very large, block letters on the signs, and use permanent, dark ink. Remember that people will be driving by your signs quickly and you want them to be noticed. Consider hanging signs near stop signs or in places where cars need to slow down.

- Decide beforehand if you want to offer any special discounts during the last hour of the sale to get rid of the leftovers.

13. LEMONADE-PLUS STAND

When the good old summertime comes around, kids will be outdoors playing—and getting hot and thirsty. Why not have some nice, cold drinks and snacks for them?

SKILLS

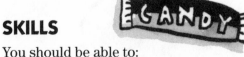

You should be able to:

- Make lemonade and other goodies.
- Count out change accurately and quickly.

TOOLS AND MATERIALS

You will need:

- A table and chair.
- Lemons and sugar (or lemonade mix) and water.

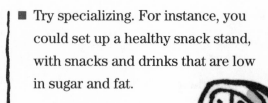

- A pitcher and cups.
- A lot of ice.
- A cooler for your ice cubes.
- Snack foods.
- Napkins.

HELPFUL HINTS

- Try to figure out what time of day is best for selling your stuff. Set up a predictable schedule if you can, so customers will be expecting you.
- Serve large portions of snacks and your best lemonade, to keep your customers coming back.
- Don't sell food that will spoil easily, unless you can keep it in a cooler.
- Find out about upcoming fairs, flea markets, and garage sales. Ask the organizer if you can set up a snack stand there.
- Expand your business to include seasonal items like iced tea in the summer, apple cider in the fall, and hot chocolate in the winter.

- Try specializing. For instance, you could set up a healthy snack stand, with snacks and drinks that are low in sugar and fat.

CUSTOMERS

- If there are baseball, soccer, or other athletic fields in your neighborhood, try setting up your table there during games.
- Other good locations are parks, busy shopping areas, and any place where there are a lot of people.
- Be sure to get permission if you want to set up a table in a park (you may need a permit from your town), or in an area that belongs to a person or business, such as a parking lot (mall management should be listed in the phone book).
- Post flyers around the neighborhood advertising your business and when it's open.

Caty's Home Baking

I started Home Baking the summer I was twelve because I wanted to have my own summer business. I got the idea for having a baked goods stand at a local farmers' market after I observed other stands such as mine at markets.

This is my third summer selling baked goods, and over the years I have adapted to suit the needs of the market. After my first few times, I had a following of faithful customers who came back week after week. I specialize in breads and cookies.

In the summer, I introduce seasonal breads such as strawberry bread and blueberry bread. The baked goods are arranged in large wire baskets that I purchased after the first season. The tables are covered in checkered cotton tablecloths, and I always have a pottery jug with fresh flowers at my stand. I have learned that presenting what you are selling well makes a difference, and conversing with your customers creates a more friendly atmosphere. Many customers are very conscious of fat content, so it's important to have various items that are low fat or fat free.

Starting a baking business is not hard. We had to get our kitchen inspected by the local health department. Also, to sell at some markets, vendors must pay a fee at the beginning of the season. I stock up on ingredients at the beginning of the season and replace them as needed as the summer progresses. I plan to make about $120 to $140 at each market that I attend during the height of the season. Of course, a young baker could "start small" by taking orders for cookies and breads and offering local delivery.

Caty Sumner, age 14

14. BACKPACK MUNCHIES

If you have snacks to sell to hungry kids right after school, you can have a pretty good business right out of your backpack!

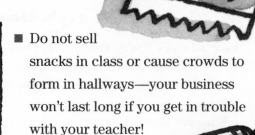

SKILLS

You need to be able to:

- Carry a heavy backpack.
- Organize your products.
- Count out change.

TOOLS AND MATERIALS

You will need:

- A backpack.
- Snacks that kids like. (Buy them in bulk at superstores or warehouse clubs.)
- Change.

HELPFUL HINTS

- Buy snacks that come in their own packages. It's not a good idea to be selling loose candy or chips.
- If the weather is hot, avoid snacks that can spoil or melt!

- Do not sell snacks in class or cause crowds to form in hallways—your business won't last long if you get in trouble with your teacher!

CUSTOMERS

- Put up signs in school, and ask your friends to help spread the word.
- Stand just outside the main door when school lets out and hand out flyers or tell everyone what you're selling.
- Try to get permission to sell snacks during after-school activities and sports events.

15. BABY-SITTING

Parents want some time to themselves now and then. A good baby-sitter is just what they need!

SKILLS

You need to be able to:

- Enjoy being around younger kids.
- Be dependable and organized.
- Be available a lot of evenings and weekends.
- Be patient.
- Know how to change a diaper.

TOOLS AND MATERIALS

You will need:

- Notebook or clipboard for keeping emergency information, dinner and bedtime instructions, and so on.
- Games or activities to do with the kids (this is optional—most kids have their own toys).
- Something to do after the kids are asleep (such as read a book, or do some homework).

References

An important tool for promoting your business is a set of references. When you have happy customers, ask them to write a letter that describes why they like your product or service. If they don't want to write a letter, ask if you can list their name and phone number as a reference. You can use these references to demonstrate the quality of your work when you meet with potential customers.

HELPFUL HINTS

- Make yourself a checklist to use when you talk to a customer, to write down bedtimes, meals, and so on. (Some parents have this written down already.) Having their bedtime written down keeps kids from trying to pull the "Our parents let us stay up till midnight!" game.

- Make sure the parents leave you emergency numbers: neighbors, grandparents, pediatrician, etc.

- Arrive at least fifteen minutes early so there's plenty of time for parents to give you instructions and show you where things are in the house.

- Ask the customers when they'll be home, so you can tell your parents. Find out how you're getting home in advance (will they drive you, or will you need to be picked up?)

- Clean up after yourself and the kids, so the house looks just as it did when you arrived.

- Ask your customers if they'd like you to do extra chores, such as washing dishes or doing laundry—for an extra fee, of course.

- Ask customers if their kids have favorite toys, books, or videos.

- Charge by the hour.

Susie Goodall
August 16th, 7 PM

✔ Bedtime 9:00
✔ Popcorn for snacktime
✔ Next door neighbor: Mrs. Smith
✔ Emergency: 911
✔ Dr. Jones: 555-1000
✔ No TV after 8:30
✔ Read bedtime story
✔ Nightlight

■ If you have the opportunity, take a first-aid class. It'll make your customers feel a lot more comfortable about leaving their kids with you!

CUSTOMERS

■ One of the best ways to find baby-sitting jobs is by word of mouth.

■ If you're just getting started, ask around your neighborhood or post signs at local preschools or day care centers.

■ Your local church, synagogue, or PTA may need a baby-sitter for services and meetings. If you can get that job, then you might be able to get more jobs with the parents who attend the meeting.

Read On!

Stuhring, Celeste, R.N.A. *Kid Sitter Basics*. Kansas City, Mo.: Westport Publishers, 1994.

16. TUTORING

Everyone needs a little help studying sometimes. Turn your school skills into a business!

SKILLS

You need to be able to:

- Enjoy being around younger kids.
- Understand and explain different kinds of information and skills.
- Be available after school and some evenings.
- Be patient.

TOOLS AND MATERIALS

You will need:

- A notebook.
- Books and other resource materials to help explain difficult topics. (Check at the library, or with the student's teacher.)

HELPFUL HINTS

- Meet with the parents of the student (and the teacher, if possible) before the first tutoring session. Find out exactly what areas their child needs help with. See if you can borrow a copy of any textbooks the student is using to see what they are covering in school.
- Write a brief progress report at the end of each session, and give it to the parents.
- Give students lots of encouragement when they make progress. Be friendly, patient, and supportive.
- Spend a little time studying the topic before you tutor the child—you'll be a better tutor if you know the subject well.
- Develop a specialty if there's a subject you're particularly good at.

CUSTOMERS

- Give flyers and business cards to teachers you know. They can recommend you to parents.
- If you are already doing jobs that put you in contact with parents, let them know that you also do tutoring.

COMPUTER ✦ ✦ BUSINESSES

17. COMPUTER CONSULTANT

Millions of people have bought home computers over the last few years, but not all of them know how to make them work. Maybe you can help them figure things out.

SKILLS

You will need to be able to:

- Understand a lot about computers.
- Explain things clearly.
- Be patient.

TOOLS AND MATERIALS

You will need:

- Your own computer, or one you have access to at all times.
- Access to computer magazines and books with helpful information.
- Blank disks.
- Troubleshooting software.

HELPFUL HINTS

- Consider having a specialty. Do you want to be a set-up-and-install ex-pert? A troubleshooter? How about an Internet guide? A software trainer? Try to match the needs of your customers with your interests and skills.
- Be professional! Make sure you know what you're doing at all stages of a job. If you don't, refer your customer to an expert, if possible. Don't take chances with your customer's valuable hardware and software.
- To learn more, find a local computer club or user group to join. Buy books on your specialty, or enroll in local classes.
- People can get confused and frustrated

by their computers—it's important to show them how to use their programs in a way that doesn't make them feel stupid.

CUSTOMERS

- Leave your business card on the front of your customers' computers so they can find your phone number as soon as something goes wrong!

- Post flyers in local computer and business supply stores.
- Advertise in school and local newspapers and community newsletters.
- Post flyers at local retirement homes and senior centers.
- Leave extra business cards and flyers with your customers so they can refer their friends and colleagues to you.

18. WORD PROCESSING AND DESKTOP PUBLISHING

If you have access to a computer and a good printer, you can make yourself very useful creating newsletters, invitations, advertisements, announcements, and more.

SKILLS

You need to be able to:

- Use a word processing or desktop publishing program.
- Type quickly and accurately.
- Check for misspelled words and incorrect grammar.
- Design newsletters, flyers, invitations, and other commonly used printed materials.
- Design your documents well.

TOOLS AND MATERIALS

You will need:

- A computer and printer.
- Word processing or desktop publishing software.
- Clip art.
- Good quality paper for printing (use different colors for variety).

HELPFUL HINTS

- Word processing usually involves retyping reports, term papers, or letters. Your job is to take your customer's rough draft and turn it into a clean, neatly printed document. Most people who do word processing charge by the page.

- Desktop publishing means designing the words in special ways to make newsletters, brochures, stationery, or other documents (often using different styles and sizes of type, adding pictures, and printing on special papers). It requires more skill and practice than word processing. You should consider charging by the hour for this service.

- You might look into purchasing a keyboarding program if you need to improve your typing speed.

- Check your work carefully for errors. Always use a spell checker, and be extra sure to read the printed version carefully as well.

- Find out when your customer needs the work finished and turn it in on time. Your customers' deadlines are very important to them.

- Collect newsletters, invitations, and other documents for design ideas.

- Discuss with your customer what style of design they'd like—elegant, fun, businesslike, or something else. Create samples of different types to show them.

CUSTOMERS

- Post your flyers at local office supply stores, copy shops, and at nearby colleges or high schools.

- Place ads in school newspapers.

- Create some examples of the work that you can do and keep them in a notebook to show potential customers. Make sure your own flyers are an example of your best work.

- Design sample flyers for businesses in your area to show them how good they'll look. Offer to post the flyers around the neighborhood as part of your services.

Read On!

Williams, Robin. *The Non-Designer's Design Book*. Berkeley, Calif.: Addison Wesley Longman, 1994.

ARTISTIC *BUSINESSES*

19. DECORATIVE PAINTING

Are you creative and artistic? Do you have the skill to paint pictures? Then you might have a career as a decorative painter!

SKILLS

You need to be able to:

- Prepare a surface to be painted.
- Set up and clean up carefully so you don't leave a mess.
- Paint nice pictures!
- Know how to use stencils.

TOOLS AND MATERIALS

You will need:

- Paints (latex or acrylics—talk to the folks at the paint store for advice).
- Brushes of various sizes.
- Rags.
- Drop cloths (plastic or fabric to protect the floor and furniture).
- Stencils.

HELPFUL HINTS

- Many painters do great things using *stencils*. These are precut patterns that are used to add decorations along the edges of ceilings, around doors, and often on furniture. You can also use stencils to decorate toys or turn small plain wooden boxes into beautiful jewelry boxes.
- If you are very good at painting pictures, you can try painting murals. These are scenes painted on the walls of a room, such as a child's bedroom. Murals can be complicated and take a lot of time, so make sure you are well prepared.
- If you are painting someone's walls, it is a *really* good idea to practice first. Buy very large sheets or rolls of paper from a crafts store and prac-

tice, practice, practice. Then try to get permission to paint your own room at home. When you are ready, *then* you can start doing decorative painting for other people.

■ Always sketch your work out on paper first. Have your customer approve your sketches and color choices before you start painting.

■ Make sure to use the right kind of paint for the job.

■ Cover furniture and floors carefully before you start.

■ Make sure the surface you are painting is clean before you begin. If the surface is very smooth, rub it with sandpaper to make sure your paint will stick.

■ Clean up splatters carefully—latex and acrylic paint will wash off with water if it hasn't dried. You'll need a special cleaner to remove splatters and drips that have hardened.

■ For extra fun, try glow-in-the-dark paint for some of the details!

CUSTOMERS

■ Create a notebook of sample paintings or designs that you can paint. Include photographs of work that you have done. It will both help your customers choose what to have you paint and show potential customers what you can do.

■ Put flyers in local decorating and paint stores. Show your wall samples at preschools, day care centers, and doctors' offices.

■ Volunteer to paint a mural at school (if they pay for your materials). Paint your business name and phone number in the corner of your painting.

■ Sell jewelry boxes and other small items at craft fairs.

Read On!

Samuelson, Alexander, editor. *Decorative Paint Finishes*. Upper Saddle River, N.J.: Creative Homeowners Press, 1996.

20. FACE PAINTING

If you have artistic skills, this can be a fun way to earn money at carnivals and fairs, and on Halloween.

SKILLS

You need to be able to:

- Paint small attractive designs!
- Be comfortable with small children.

TOOLS AND MATERIALS

You will need:

- Face paints (special paints that are safe for the skin).
- Glitter.
- Small brushes.
- Small makeup sponges (available in drugstores).
- Water for rinsing your brushes.
- A mirror for customers to check out your work!
- A table and chairs.
- A drop cloth if you are working indoors.

HELPFUL HINTS

- Set up examples of the pictures you do on a display board for kids to choose from.
- Make sure your sample pictures include popular images such as smiley faces, rainbows, and balloons. And don't forget dinosaurs, soccer balls, and superheroes!
- Practice at home on your family and friends.

CUSTOMERS

- You can set up a booth at special events like festivals and parades. Have your business card available, and make sure it says that you're available for birthday parties.
- Do full-face painting to help create Halloween costumes—animals, clowns, ghouls, and vampires!
- Advertise in places parents take little kids—preschools, day care centers, swimming pools, and outside toy stores.

Read On!

Face Painting. Palo Alto, Calif.: Klutz Press, 1990.

21. GREETING CARDS

Sending greeting cards is a very popular tradition. If you have artistic ability, this may be the business for you.

SKILLS

You need to be able to:

- Design attractive cards.
- Paint or draw them—or design them on your computer.

TOOLS AND MATERIALS

You will need:

- Blank cards and envelopes. Check craft stores and stationery stores to buy these, or make your own from nice paper.
- Paint, pens, brushes, rubber stamps, glitter, and so on—or a computer and color printer.

HELPFUL HINTS

- If you want to duplicate a design, check local print shops and copy centers for the best deal on printing your cards. The more cards you print, the less each one will cost.

- Explore specialty cards—animal cards to sell at the pet store, flower cards to sell at the nursery, and so forth. Use your imagination!
- Come up with clever sayings for the inside, or just leave the inside blank.
- If you make your own cards, buy the envelopes first, so you can be sure your cards will fit in the envelopes.

CUSTOMERS

- Show samples of your cards at school a few weeks before major holidays.
- Post flyers with sample cards attached, in strategic places: Christmas cards at churches, Mother's Day and Father's Day cards at day care centers, and Valentine's Day and friendship cards at elementary, junior high, and high schools.
- See if local card and gift shops, bookstores, newsstands, and toy stores

will carry your cards, either by buy-ing them from you or selling them on consignment.

■ Print the name of your business and contact information on the back of your cards.

Read On!

Hauser, Priscilla. *Create Your Own Greeting Cards & Gift Wrap*. Cincin-nati, Ohio: North Light Books, 1994.

22. JEWELRY

Do you have a flair for design? If you can create attractive jewelry that you like to wear, then there's a good chance you can sell it, too!

SKILLS

You need to be able to:

■ Handle small beads and jewelry pieces.

■ Attractively mix and match colors and patterns.

■ Know how to attach fasteners.

TOOLS AND MATERIALS

You will need:

■ Beads, charms, or other pretty items.

■ Earring posts, necklace clasps, and brooch pins. You can buy these at craft stores.

■ Thin wire or cord.

- A needle for threading beads.
- Needle-nose pliers for crimping.
- Containers with small compartments for keeping your supplies organized.
- Display cards or racks. Check craft stores or make your own.

HELPFUL HINTS

- Make sure you schedule a regular time for making your jewelry. It takes time and work, and you can't sell it if you don't make it!
- Check local stores to see what styles are popular.
- Try to create your own special kind of jewelry. Show samples to your friends to see if they like them.
- Look for classes on making jewelry at your local craft store, community center, school, or summer camp. You can learn new ideas and skills to improve your products and sales.
- Think about your target market. Are you selling colorful necklaces and friendship bracelets to kids, or elegant (and more expensive) items for adults? Make sure to match your style of jewelry with your type of customer.

CUSTOMERS

- There are many kinds of gift fairs and bazaars for people who sell crafts such as this. Find ones that charge low fees that you can afford.
- Attach tags to your jewelry with your business's name and phone number, so customers can come back for more.
- Approach local gift shops to see if they will sell your jewelry. Call and make an appointment to meet with the shop manager, and bring samples of your work. If they are interested in selling more than one or two pieces, offer them a price break.
- Check to see if you can put up a display at your school, or set up a table at a school fair.
- Make flyers with photos of your jewelry attached.

Read On!

Fitch, Janet. *The Art and Craft of Jewelry*. San Francisco: Chronicle Books, 1994.

Grape, Carol. *Handmade Jewelry: Simple Steps to Creating Wearable Art*. Cincinnati, Ohio: North Light Books, 1996.

23. PUPPETS

Puppets can be made of fabric, papier-mâché, wood, or other materials. You can put on puppet shows or sell your puppets—or both!

SKILLS

You need to be able to:

- Design appealing puppets.
- Safely use a sewing machine.
- Sculpt faces, hands, and other parts.

TOOLS AND MATERIALS

You will need:

- Scissors, glue, and paints.
- Sewing machine, fabric, and thread.
- Papier-mâché for hands and faces.
- Buttons and other objects for eyes, decorations, etc.

HELPFUL HINTS

- Check out different kinds of puppets in toy stores for ideas.
- Sketch your designs first and make paper patterns to see how they look.
- Attach the fabrics and details firmly, so your puppets don't fall apart.
- Try creating one or two puppet characters and making different variations of them around a theme, such as sports or jobs.
- You can expand your business to include dolls, teddy bears, and other stuffed animals.
- Specialize. Decide how elaborate you want your puppets to be, based on what styles appeal to you and what materials are readily available.

CUSTOMERS

- Get a booth at a craft fair.
- Talk to local gift and toy shops about selling your puppets.
- Put together puppet shows at the library or your school and sell your puppets after each performance.

- Make sure all the puppets you sell have tags with your business name and contact information.

Read On!

Henson, Cheryl. *The Muppets Make Puppets!* New York: Workman Publishing, 1994.

24. BUTTONS

For some reason, people just love to wear buttons with cute pictures and special sayings on them. The good news for your business is that they aren't all that hard to make!

SKILLS

You need to be able to:

- Design unique buttons.
- Follow directions for using a button maker (it takes a little practice).

TOOLS AND MATERIALS

You will need:

- Scissors.
- Cardboard.

- Glue and tape.
- Safety pins.
- A computer and color printer for printing words and pictures for the buttons, or pens and pencils for drawing your designs and access to a photocopier.
- A button maker (optional). You can buy them for $60 to $110 from craft stores and catalogs.

HELPFUL HINTS

■ Design interesting buttons to appeal to your target market—sheriff's badges for little kids, team spirit buttons for sports fans, etc. Your designs can be made of words, drawings, photographs, or even magazine clippings.

■ The easiest way to make a button is to glue a picture to cardboard (make sure to trim it carefully) and attach a safety pin to the back with tape.

■ If you expect to sell a lot of buttons, you may want to invest in a button maker, to easily make professional-quality buttons. A button maker permanently mounts a picture onto a metal backing under a protective layer of plastic. It can be a little tricky to learn, so expect to throw away a few buttons when you first start. Once you get the hang of it, though, you can make a button in about a minute!

■ Make sample buttons and take orders based on your samples. That way you can make just as many as you need. Or make buttons specially for each customer while they wait.

■ *Safety note*: Buttons have very sharp pins in the back. Do not sell them to kids younger than second grade without their parents' permission.

CUSTOMERS

■ Wear your own buttons as advertisements!

■ Put small stickers with your business name and contact information on the backs of the buttons.

■ Sell buttons to local businesses, which they can use to promote themselves.

■ If you have an instant camera, you can sell buttons to people at fairs with their own pictures in them.

25. BIRD FEEDERS

Grown-ups just love to feed birds, so bird feeders have been popular for a long time. They might even be popular enough to support a small business!

SKILLS

You need to be able to:

- Read and understand the bird feeder building plans you choose.
- Have some experience with basic woodworking.

- Get an adult to help you with sawing and drilling wood.
- Use a hammer and nails.

TOOLS AND MATERIALS

You will need:

- Wood (check the building plans for the correct type and size to use).
- Building plans.
- Hammer and small nails.
- Saw and drill (do not use without adult help).
- Glue and caulk.
- Paint and brushes.
- Sandpaper.
- Hooks for hanging bird feeders.

HELPFUL HINTS

- Sawing, drilling, and hammering can be dangerous. Ask an adult to help you, and work carefully.
- Measure carefully before you start.
- Look for books that have plans and detailed material lists for building bird feeders.
- Decorative bird feeders (in the shapes of houses, stores, lighthouses, and so on) can be very popular. Be creative!
- Consider expanding your business to make bat houses and bee homes, too!

CUSTOMERS

- Sell your bird feeders through local gardening stores, gardening clubs, and craft stores.
- Put flyers at pet stores and veterinarians' offices. (You're looking for animal lovers!)
- Make sure the name of your business and contact information is on your bird feeders.
- Put them out in your own front yard as an advertisement!

Read On!

Newton-Cox, Andrew, and Deena Beverley. *Making Birdhouses*. New York: Anness Publishers, 1998.

Baldwin, Edward A. *Building Birdhouses and Feeders*. Edited by Norman Rae. San Ramon, Calif.: Meredith Books, 1990.

Tuttle, Merlin D., and Donna L. Hensley. *Bat House Builder's Handbook*. Austin: University of Texas Press, 1997.

26. YARD SIGNS

Yard signs are big, wooden signs posted in front of a house that are a fun way of announcing special events. For instance, it can be a stork and say IT'S A GIRL! or be a big cake that says HAPPY BIRTH-DAY, FRANK! You can rent a sign to a customer for a few days or a week, or make a sign specially for someone who wants to keep it.

SKILLS

You need to be able to:
- Saw wood (get an adult to help you).
- Paint well.
- Design appealing signs.

TOOLS AND MATERIALS

You will need:
- Wood (outdoor plywood is treated so the rain won't ruin it).
- Outdoor paints and brushes.
- A jigsaw or saber saw and a drill (do not use without adult help).
- A post to stick in the ground.
- Sandpaper.
- Screws and a screwdriver.

HELPFUL HINTS

- Pick just a few ideas to start with, such as baby announcements and birthdays.
- Leave a spot on your sign where the lettering can be changed—a card hanging from the stork's mouth, a space on the side of a big cake, and so on. This way you can rent the sign out again after the customer is finished with it.
- Sketch out your ideas first. Make small models with cardboard to see how they look.

- Make your signs big— about three or four feet tall. You want people driving by to see them!
- Carefully attach the sign to a post with a hammer and nails. Drive the post into the ground.

CUSTOMERS

■ Hand out flyers at gift shops, greeting card stores, and party supply stores.

■ Put signs in your own front yard that advertise your business.

■ Distribute flyers and pictures of your signs to parents of young children— at school events, day care centers, and in your neighborhood. A sign can be a fun addition to their child's birthday party.

27. HOUSE BANNERS

Banners are popular decorating items on houses. They hang from flagpoles and have colorful designs that can be changed during the year. If you can sew them, you can sell them, too!

SKILLS

You need to be able to:

■ Operate a sewing machine.

■ Design attractive banners.

TOOLS AND MATERIALS

You will need:

■ A sewing machine.

■ Nylon fabric in a variety of colors.

■ Appropriate thread in various colors.

■ Patterns for different banners.

■ Fabric paints.

HELPFUL HINTS

■ Sketch out your designs on paper first.

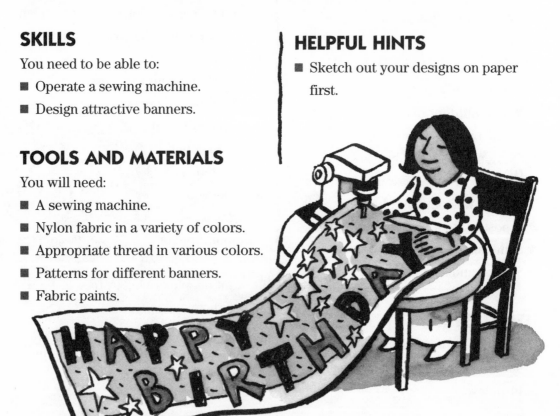

- Banners can be made for different holidays, seasons, and celebrations like birthdays. Be creative!
- Look around your neighborhood and in gardening and variety stores to see what kinds of banners and designs are popular and how they are made. Then create your own variations and new ideas so you will stand out from the competition.
- To hang your banner, fold over the top two inches of fabric. Sew it down to form a sleeve across the entire top of the banner. Then take a long wooden stick about an inch thick (from a hardware or craft store) and put it through the sleeve. Tie a piece of rope securely to both ends of the stick, and hang it from a hook or nail.

CUSTOMERS

- Post flyers (or banners) at gift shops and home stores.
- See if local businesses want to buy banners to use to promote themselves.
- Use a banner to advertise in your own front yard.

28. T-SHIRTS

If you are an artist, you probably like it when people appreciate your work. What better compliment than for them to wear your art—and pay for it, too!

SKILLS

You need to be able to:

- Create interesting, attractive designs.
- Paint, silk-screen, and/or embroider your shirts.

TOOLS AND MATERIALS

You will need:

- Plain T-shirts of different sizes.
- Paints. (Check the craft store for the different kinds made especially for painting fabric.)
- Extra items to jazz up your shirts (sequins, beads, etc.).

- If you decide to silk-screen instead of paint, you will need screen material, a screen frame, a squeegee, stencil materials, and fabric inks.

HELPFUL HINTS

- Go to clothing stores and see what's popular. Then get creative and come up with something unique!
- Test your ideas by making single copies for yourself and seeing what people think.

Chad's T-shirt Design

Our school booster club wanted our school to have a wider variety of clothing featuring our mascot, the Hornet. I was asked to draw some hornets for this project. I did, and we took the six drawings to a local shop that uses computer technology to decorate T-shirts, sweatshirts, and baseball hats.

My designs were a success. Two weeks later I got a call from the shop asking me to draw some T-Birds. With each purchase featuring my design, I would get ten percent in return.

Recently, I received my first check, for twenty dollars. Now the school staff members are discussing plans to make my designs their official staff shirts.

This is not a bad start in a career!

Chad Zdroik, age 14

- Look for design ideas from within your community. For instance, make shirts with the school mascot (with permission, of course), the name of your town, or pictures of a local landmark.
- Buy good-quality cotton T-shirts, in bulk packages if possible.
- Run a few sample shirts through the washing machine a couple times to be sure the fabric paints and any items you attached stay put. Your customers will be glad to know the shirts are machine washable.
- If you get a lot of orders, explore paying a silk-screening company to make the shirts. While it will be more expensive than making them yourself, you may be able to use fancier designs.
- Consider expanding your business to include sweatshirts, caps, tote bags, and mugs.

CUSTOMERS

- Wear samples of your work when you go out. When someone admires your shirt, offer to sell him or her one just like it!
- See if there are any clothing stores nearby that will sell your shirts.
- Get permission to set up a booth at craft shows and sporting events.
- Try to sell custom-designed T-shirts to small groups, such as birthday parties, school clubs, and sports teams.

29. FLOWER BOXES

Flowers will brighten up any home or apartment. Sell flower boxes to spread some color!

SKILLS

You need to be able to:

- Raise plants from seed or small seedlings.
- Choose colors and types of plants that will look good together.

TOOLS AND MATERIALS

You will need:

- Planter boxes or pots.
- Flower seeds and/or small seedlings.
- Potting soil.
- Fertilizer.
- Sunny location.

HELPFUL HINTS

- It takes four to six weeks to get plants started from seed. Check the back of the seed packages to see when to plant them and how to care for the plants.
- If you haven't got the time or the room to grow from seed, buy your flowers early in the season when they're still small. That's when they're least expensive.
- Plant a mixture of tall and low flowers. Add some leafy plants (such as ivy) for variety.

- You can make small plantings in terra-cotta flowerpots. Paint the flowerpots for added value.
- Try specializing in wildflowers, herbs, or vegetables.

CUSTOMERS

- Sell your flower boxes at the local farmers' market. (You will probably need to reserve and pay for your space.)
- Advertise at local plant shops, florists, gift shops, and at school.
- Have your business cards laminated (sealed in plastic) and attach them to the back of the boxes or pots.

Read On!

Phillips, Sue, and Neil Sutherland. *A Creative Step-by-Step Guide to Container Gardening.* North Vancouver, British Columbia: Whitecap Books, Ltd., 1994.

30. KEY CHAINS AND ZIPPER PULLS

These are more than just useful—they're popular, too!
Especially if you can make them and sell them!

SKILLS

You need to be able to:

- Work with your hands.
- Be creative!

TOOLS AND MATERIALS

You will need:

- Key chain clips.
- Small hooks that attach easily to standard-size zippers.
- Plastic modeling compound (such as Sculpey or Fimo).
- Small charms or craft items.

HELPFUL HINTS

- Check out the key chains at local auto supply stores and gift shops. See what's popular.
- Think about your target market. For example, some kids may like key chains and zipper pulls with animal figures attached. Adults may want craft items that represent hobbies or jobs (like little gardening tools, fishing bobbers, cars, etc.)
- Buy your key chain clips in bulk at a hardware store or crafts store, to keep your costs down.
- Look for decorations that can easily be attached to a key ring or zipper—or make them yourself out of ribbons, lanyard, buttons, and other objects.
- Whatever you attach to the key chain has to be sturdy—it's going to get banged around in someone's pocket or purse a lot! For zipper pulls, items should be smaller and lighter.

CUSTOMERS

- Hang your own key chains or zipper pulls off your jacket or backpack. When people admire them, offer to sell them!
- If you make specialty key chains or zipper pulls, try to find specialty stores that will carry them (sports key chains at sport stores, etc.).

PART 3

TAKING CARE OF BUSINESS WITH THE KIDBIZ DISK

Your book came with a computer disk that has special files to help you run your business. The software will give you tools to track your finances, market your business, and keep good records. It's important to pay attention to the details—they are a big part of being successful!

The KidBiz disk can help your business take off. This section will show you how to:

✓ Install the KidBiz disk

✓ Create a spreadsheet

✓ Save, print, and exit your spreadsheet

✓ Restart the program and edit your spreadsheet

✓ Open and modify the template files

✓ Make your own advertising flyers, print advertisements, letterhead, and business cards

✓ Create invoices, contracts, accounting forms, and customer lists

THE KIDBIZ SPREAD-SHEET PROGRAM: Tracking Revenue and Expenses

You can use the spreadsheet program on the KidBiz disk to estimate your revenue, expenses, and profit—before you even start your business. Once your business is up and running, you can make a new spreadsheet using your *actual* revenue and expenses. Did you make a profit? How does it compare to your estimated profit? By keeping track of the money coming into your business and going out of it, you'll be able to figure out the best answer to things like:

• How much to charge for your goods and services.

• How you can save money by reducing expenses

• Which products or services generate the most revenue.

So how do you use a spreadsheet? It's not that difficult. . . .

USING THE KIDBIZ SPREADSHEET PROGRAM

To start the program, follow these steps:

STEP 1: Install the program

If you have Windows 95:

• Put the disk in the disk drive.

• Click on the *Start* button. Choose *Run* from the menu.

• The *Run* window will appear. Type the following into the box:
A:\setup.exe
and click *OK*.

• This will start a program to install the KidBiz spreadsheet and templates (see page 98). It will ask you a question or two while it is installing. Just

Welcome screen

click *Continue* to go on, and installation will be completed.

• Click on the red KidBiz icon to open the spreadsheet.

If you have Windows 3.1:
- Put the disk in the disk drive.
- Choose *File* from the Program Manager menu bar. Choose *Run* from the menu.
- The *Run* window will appear. Type the following into the box: A:\Setup.exe
- This will start a program to install the KidBiz spreadsheet and templates (see page 98). It will ask you a question or two while it is installing. Just click *Continue* to go on, and installation will be completed.
- Click on the red KidBiz icon to open the spreadsheet.

STEP 2: Create a new spreadsheet.

When the program starts up, you will be given the choice to *Create Spreadsheet* or *Open Spreadsheet* (one you've already started). Click on *Create Spreadsheet*.

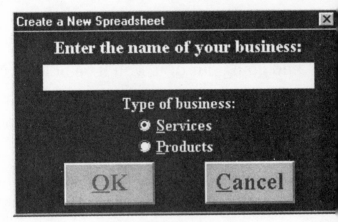

Create a new spreadsheet

STEP 3: Choose your business.

On the next screen you will need to do three things:
- Type in the name of your company.
- Choose the kind of business you are doing—do you sell a *service* (such as dog-walking or baby-sitting) or a *product* (such as lemonade or T-shirts)?
- Click *OK*.

STEP 4: Enter your revenue.

If you choose to create a spreadsheet for a **product business**, the next screen will look like this (except yours won't have any information in it yet).

• Type in the names of the items that you sell into the blank lines under "Products sold."

• In the next column, under "sale price," enter how much you charge for each item.

• Click in the boxes labeled "Month 1," "Month 2," and "Month 3," and fill in the actual months that match your business. (Or, if you want, you could put other times in these boxes, such

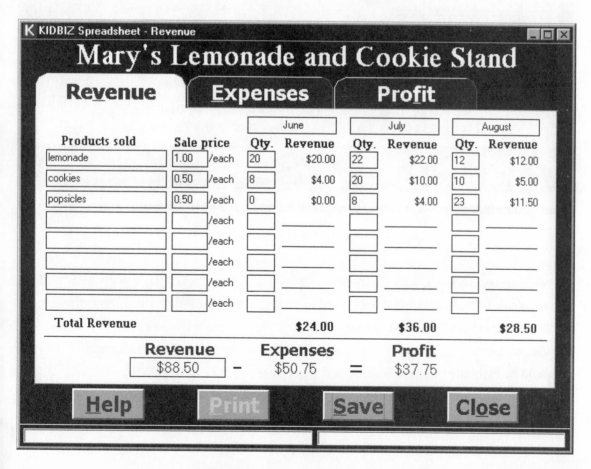

K KIDBIZ Spreadsheet - Revenue										

Mary's Lemonade and Cookie Stand

Re_v_enue **_E_xpenses** **Pro_f_it**

Products sold	Sale price		June Qty.	Revenue	July Qty.	Revenue	August Qty.	Revenue
lemonade	1.00	/each	20	$20.00	22	$22.00	12	$12.00
cookies	0.50	/each	8	$4.00	20	$10.00	10	$5.00
popsicles	0.50	/each	0	$0.00	8	$4.00	23	$11.50
		/each						
		/each						
		/each						
		/each						
		/each						
Total Revenue				**$24.00**		**$36.00**		**$28.50**

Revenue		Expenses		Profit
$88.50	−	$50.75	=	$37.75

Help   **Print**   **Save**   **Close**

Revenue screen—product business

Revenue screen—service business

as Monday, Tuesday, and Wednesday, or Week 1, Week 2, Week 3. Use whatever works best for your business.)

• Enter the quantity of each item you sold or estimate you will sell in each month into the "Qty" columns.

If you choose to create a spreadsheet for a **service business**, the revenue screen will look like this (except yours won't have any information in it yet).

- Type in the names of the people that you work for into the blank lines under "Name of customer."

- Click in the boxes labeled "Month 1," "Month 2," and "Month 3," and fill in the actual months that match your business. (Or, if you want, you could put other times in these boxes, such as Monday, Tuesday, and Wednesday, or Week 1, Week 2, Week 3. Use whatever works best for your business.)

- Then fill in the rate you charge for each hour you work, and the number of hours you worked each month. If you want to charge by the day, or by the job, just click on the word "hour" to change it, then hit *Enter*.

The computer will do the rest for you! The program will total up your revenue for each month, and will calculate your total revenue for the three-month period.

That revenue probably looks pretty good! Unfortunately, though, we can't stop there—we have to enter in your *expenses*, too.

STEP 5: Enter your expenses.

- Click on the *Expenses* tab on the top of the spreadsheet. Now you will have a screen that looks something like the sample on the following page.

- Type in each of your supplies and other expenses on the lines provided.

KIDBIZ Spreadsheet - Expenses

Mary's Lemonade and Cookie Stand

Revenue   Expenses   Profit

Supplies and other expenses	Cost		June Qty.	Expense	July Qty.	Expense	August Qty.	Expense
lemons	0.20	/each	30	$6.00	30	$6.00	20	$4.00
sugar	1.50	/each	1	$1.50			1	$1.50
pitcher	5.00	/each	1	$5.00				_____
paper cups	1.50	/each	1	$1.50	1	$1.50		_____
napkins	2.00	/each	1	$2.00				_____
cookies	0.25	/each	10	$2.50	25	$6.25	10	$2.50
juice	2.50	/each		_____	1	$2.50	2	$5.00
popsicle trays	3.00	/each		_____	1	$3.00		_____
Total Expenses				**$18.50**		**$19.25**		**$13.00**

Revenue		Expenses		Profit
$88.50	−	$50.75	=	$37.75

Help   Print   Save   Close

Expenses screen

- Fill in how much each one cost per item in the box next to it.
- Next, enter the total quantity of each supply you purchased during each month in the boxes in the month columns.
- If you buy things in bulk (such as a box of cookies), enter the price for one box in the "Cost" column, and the number of boxes (not the number of cookies) in the quantity column.

Once you've entered all your costs and prices, the spreadsheet will calculate your total expenses. It will then automatically calculate your profit!

If the box under the word "Profit" has a number that is black, then you made money! If it's a red, negative number, however, then you haven't made a profit—you've got a loss. Try out some different numbers to figure out the best way to increase your revenue or reduce your expenses.

STEP 6: Your profit summary.

The third and final tab on your spreadsheet is the *Profit* tab. Go ahead and click on this tab now. There isn't any information for you to enter here—just a summary of the information you've already entered in the other screens.

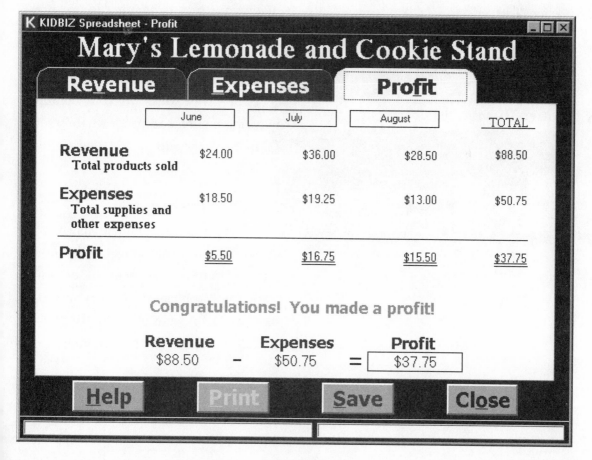

KIDBIZ Spreadsheet - Profit

Mary's Lemonade and Cookie Stand

	June	July	August	TOTAL
Revenue Total products sold	$24.00	$36.00	$28.50	$88.50
Expenses Total supplies and other expenses	$18.50	$19.25	$13.00	$50.75
Profit	$5.50	$16.75	$15.50	$37.75

Congratulations! You made a profit!

Revenue		Expenses		Profit
$88.50	−	$50.75	=	$37.75

Help   Print   Save   Close

Profit screen

Saving your spreadsheet.

It's very important to save your spreadsheet frequently. To do this, simply click the *Save* button. You'll get a screen that looks like the picture below.

The name of your business will appear in the box. This is the name to look for the next time you want to use this spreadsheet. Click *OK* and your spreadsheet is saved.

Save screen

Printing your spreadsheet.

To print your spreadsheet, just press the *Print* button. This will bring you to the "Print Preview" screen, which shows you what the printout will look like. Now press *Print* again. That's it! Press the *Close* button to return to the main program.

If you have printing problems, check your printer manual to be sure your printer is properly connected. Then check your Windows printer settings and make sure your printer is properly set up as your default printer. (Refer to Windows Help for more information on how to do this.)

Exiting the program

When you are finished, save your spreadsheet, then click on the *Close* button to return to the "Welcome" screen. From there, you can start a new spreadsheet, work on an existing one, or press the *Exit* button to quit the program.

Starting the program again

The next time you want to use the spreadsheet, just follow these directions (you won't need the disk).

If you are using Windows 95:
- Click the *Start* button on the bottom of your screen.
- Move your cursor to "Programs." Then click on the KidBiz menu item and then the KidBiz icon. The Welcome screen will appear.

If you are using Windows 3.1:
- Click in the KidBiz program group window, which you will see on your screen.
- Click on the KidBiz icon. The Welcome screen will appear.

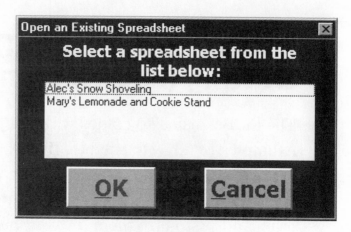

Open an Existing Spreadsheet screen

Editing your spreadsheet

From the Welcome screen, click on the button that says "Open Spreadsheet." Click on the name of the spreadsheet that you want to work on to highlight it. Then click on the *OK* button. That's all there is to it. (Just remember to save any changes you make!)

Using the on-line help

If you get stuck, click on the *Help* button to get tips and instructions!

THE KIDBIZ TEMPLATES: Getting (and Keeping) Customers

The KidBiz disk also comes with *templates*. These are ready-made examples of advertisements, flyers, invoices, and other business forms. Some of them are for *marketing* and some are for *record keeping*. You can bring these files into your word processing program and customize them for your business. Let's look at how you can use them.

MARKETING TEMPLATES

To learn how to use the templates, we'll start by making an advertising flyer.

STEP 1. If you haven't installed the Kid-Biz disk already, follow STEP 1 on pages 89–90 to install the disk, but do not open the spreadsheet. Find the flyer template and click on it to open it.

STEP 2. If you installed the disk earlier, you do not need to use the disk again. For Windows 95, just click the *Start* button on the bottom of your screen. Click "Programs," then click "KidBiz." If you are using Windows 3.1, click on the KidBiz window icon on your screen. Find the flyer template and click on it to open it.

ALEC'S
Snow Shoveling
SNOW PROBLEM?
No problem!

We clear driveways
and sidewalks
so you don't have to!

Fast, efficient service

Available early mornings,
afternoons, and weekends

Call 555-1234

Flyer template

Note: After you install the disk, you can also open the flyer template by going to the *File* menu and choosing *Open*. Then find and double-click on the file c:/Kidbiz/Template/Flyer.

You will have a document on your screen that looks like the one on the previous page. You need to make a few changes to it (unless your name is Alec and you plan to run a snow-shoveling business!).

STEP 3. First you will need to replace the picture with one that is appropriate to your business. Click once on the picture, and you'll see little black squares appear at the corners. (They're called "handles.") Hit the delete key to remove the art. Don't worry, it will still be saved in the original template.

STEP 4. If you are using Microsoft Word, click on the *Insert* menu at the top of the screen. When the menu drops down, click on *Picture*. Then click on "ClipArt."

If you are using WordPerfect, go to the *Graphics* menu at the top and click on it. Then click on *Figure*. You will see a box with a list of clip art files.

Note: In addition to this clip art there are many art choices available. You can copy and paste a different piece of art from one of the other templates. You can buy a CD-Rom with thousands of pieces of clip art for as little as five dollars. Or you can download clip art for free from many internet web sites. (See p. 107 for a couple of recommended web sites.)

STEP 5. Choose the picture that you want to use and insert it into the template. If you need to make it larger or smaller, click and hold down on one of the little squares in the corners or sides of the picture. Then drag the corner or side *out* to make the image bigger, or *in* to make it smaller. You can also drag the picture to move it exactly where you want it. This takes some practice, so be patient!

STEP 6. Once you have made the picture the right size, then it's time to change the text. Drag your cursor over the business name on the flyer and highlight it. Then type in your own business name. Next, do the same thing with the business description and other text.

Make sure you make it sound really interesting! (For some templates in WordPerfect, you'll need to double-click on the text area in order to add or change text.)

STEP 7. After you've finished writing, go up to the *Tools* menu and choose *Spelling* (or *Speller*). Always check the spelling in your marketing materials!

STEP 8. When you're done, go to the *File* menu and select *Save As*. Give your flyer a name that you can remember.

STEP 9. To print your flyer, go to the *File* menu again and choose *Print*. Congratulations! Your first business flyer!

You can use the other templates in the same way. There are files for print advertisements, letterhead, and business cards.

All your templates are carefully designed. You can change the layout, font style and size, or anything else you want. Just be careful (especially with the business card template) because it's easy to push things around and have the cards, newsletters, or other documents print out the wrong size.

The good news is that because the file on the disk is a *template*, you can't make any permanent changes to the original template. So if your experiment doesn't work, you can just start over again.

The **print advertisement** looks like the one below.

Print advertisement template

The **letterhead** looks like this:

Letterhead template

Once you replace the picture and text, you can print it out and take it to your local or school newspaper.

After you replace the text, you can use it for writing professional business letters. To make it look even better, print it out on some of the nice paper that you can get at an office supply or computer store.

The **business card** template will look like this when you open it up:

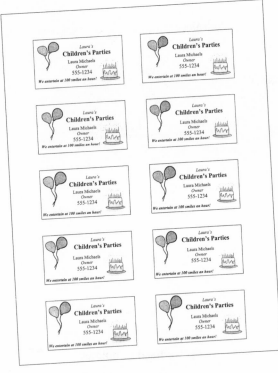

Business card template

You'll see ten business cards. Go ahead and change the picture and text for each of them.

Make sure you spell-check and save your file. Then print out your cards and cut them out. Look for nice heavy paper at the office supply or computer store to add a little pizzazz to your cards.

RECORD-KEEPING TEMPLATES

There are five templates that you can use to help you keep your business in order. They can each be changed to match your business, just as the marketing materials could.

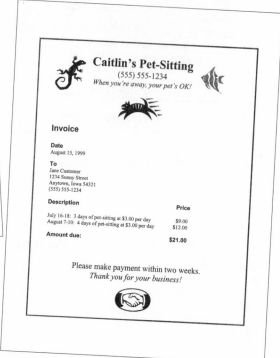

Invoice template

An **invoice** is a form asking the customer to pay for your service after you are done. (It is also called a bill.)

Fill in the sections with your hourly fee and the number of hours you spent on the job. Multiply out the total, fill it in, and print it out. Sign the bottom and give it to your customer.

A **contract** is a written agreement with someone. If you do a service for a customer, or you decide to work together with someone else in your business, even if it's your best friend, it is a good idea to have a contract.

Accounting

Company name: _____

Date: _____

List each product or service you sell: Revenue

_____   _____
_____   _____
_____   _____
_____   _____
_____   _____
_____   _____
_____   _____

                                        Total: $ _____

List each item you buy: Expenses

_____   _____
_____   _____
_____   _____
_____   _____
_____   _____
_____   _____

                                        Total: $ _____

Attach receipts here:

Accounting template

LAURA'S CHILDREN'S PARTIES
555-1234
We entertain at 100 smiles an hour!

Contract

June 23, 1999

Emmett Fitz
704 Pin Oak Rd.
Smallville, Nebraska 18124

Services/products to be provided

Laura's Children's Parties will provide the following services/products to **Emmett Fitz**: Birthday party for 12 boys, including:
• Twelve sets of party favors
• Decorated cake and vanilla ice cream
• Paper plates, plastic utensils, and cups
• Party decorations for dining room and play room with a baseball theme
• Games and entertainment for two hours
• Clean-up at the end of the party

Date of delivery

Laura's Children's Parties will provide the services/products described above on July 4, 1999, from 1:00 P.M. until 4:00 P.M.

Payment

The cost for the above services/products is sixty dollars. Payment is due at completion.

Signed:

_____   _____
Laura Michaels, Laura's Children's Parties   Date

_____   _____
Customer   Date

Contract template

The **accounting** form is useful for tracking your expenses and revenue every day that you work.

It has lines for you to enter your income and expenses, and a place to staple any receipts. You can use the information from these forms for filling out your spreadsheet.

The **customer list** is a place for you to keep information about your customers, including name, address, phone number, and some brief notes about them.

This kind of a list is helpful even when you have just a few customers. And if you start having a lot, it can be a *lifesaver*!

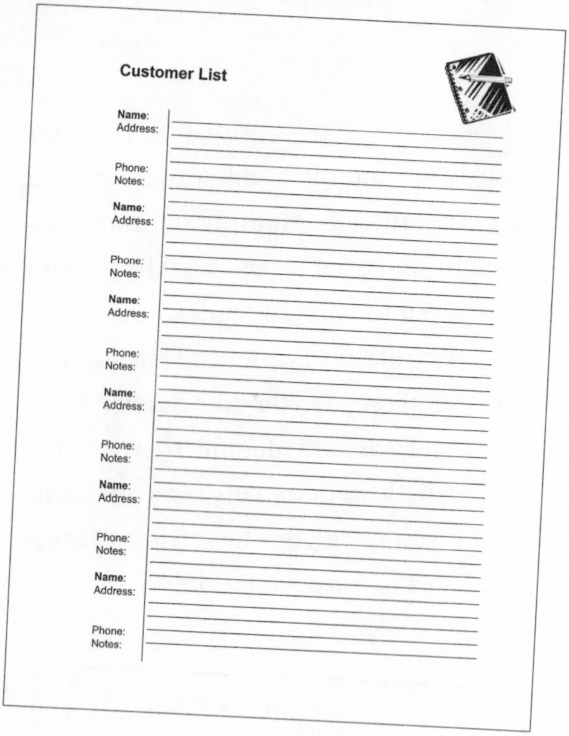

Customer List

Name:
Address:

Phone:
Notes:

Name:
Address:

Phone:
Notes:

Name:
Address:

Phone:
Notes:

Name:
Address:

Phone:
Notes:

Name:
Address:

Phone:
Notes:

Name:
Address:

Phone:
Notes:

Customer list template

TIME TO TAKE OFF!

This is it—time to give it a try. Do your best to put together a great business. Check the details (then check them again) and go for it. If your business is an immediate success, congratulations! If it isn't, *don't give up*. Many famous business owners had one, two, even three or more failures before they found the right path. If you have trouble, stick it out. You'll get there eventually.

Most important of all, HAVE FUN!

GLOSSARY

Accounting: Keeping track of all the income and expenses of a business.

Advertising: Getting information about your business to customers through flyers, business cards, printed announcements, T-shirts, or whatever works.

Biodegradable: Products or materials that will eventually decompose after they are discarded. These are less of an environmental problem than non-biodegradable items such as plastic.

Bottom line: The total profit or loss for your business.

Budget: A plan for how much money you will spend and earn.

Bulk: A large amount of something. It is usually a good idea to buy supplies in bulk to save money.

Business: An organized effort to earn money by providing services or selling products (or both).

Business card: A small card with the name and contact information for a business.

Business plan: The goals and budget used to make sure a business makes a profit.

Competition: Businesses that sell similar products or services.

Consignment: An arrangement where a store will try to sell your product for you, in exchange for part of the revenue from the sale. Whatever they don't sell, they will return to you.

Contract: A written agreement between two or more people. It is an important way to make sure everyone understands the rules at the beginning of a business.

Customer: A person who buys a product or service.

Desktop publishing: Using a computer to prepare printed materials with graphics, such as newsletters, advertisements, and flyers.

Employee: Someone who is paid to work for a business.

Entrepreneur: A person who runs a business—that's you!

Estimate: A careful guess about the amount of money you will spend or receive.

Expenses: The money that a business spends.

Finances: The revenue, expenses, and loans of a business.

Flyer: A single-page advertisement that can be distributed through local shops, door-to-door, and posted on bulletin boards.

Inventory: The supplies and materials that a business has on hand.

Invoice: A list of products sold and their prices. Also called a *bill*.

Loan: Money that one person (say, your mom) gives to another person (you, for instance) that will be paid back.

Loss: The money owed when expenses are more than revenue. The opposite of a profit.

Marketing: Advertising and selling a product or service.

Nontoxic: A material that isn't dangerous or poisonous.

Partnership: An agreement between two or more people to work together in a business.

Product: An item sold by a business.

Profit: The money made by a business when revenue is more than expenses. A much happier word than *loss*.

Recycled: Made from materials that have been used before. This helps reduce the amount of natural resources used and trash thrown away.

References: People who will recommend you to new customers.

Revenue: The money that a business collects. Also called *income*.

Service: A skill or labor sold by a business.

Spreadsheet: A program for helping with accounting that does automatic calculations.

Superstore: A very large store that usually has a wide selection and lower prices.

Target market: The specific group of customers that you are trying to sell to, such as kids, or dog owners, or young women who buy jewelry.

Template: A computer file that can be used to create a new, customized document without affecting the original file.

Word processing: Using a computer to write, edit, and print documents.

RESOURCES

Aaseng, Nathan. *The Problem Solvers: People Who Turned Problems into Products*. Minneapolis, Minn.: Lerner Publications, 1989.

Entrepreneurship Institute
3592 Corporate Drive
Columbus, OH 43231
(614) 895-1153

International Directory of Young Entrepreneurs
3905 Lake Vista Court
Encino, CA 91316
(800) 455-4393

Junior Achievement, Inc.
One Education Way
Colorado Springs, CO 80906
(719) 540-8000
http://www.ja.org

Kids Venture: How to Start Your Own Business (video). Available from Media Crafters Limited, 7201 Haven Avenue, Suite E-325, Alta Loma, CA 91701.

NASCO Arts and Crafts Catalog
4825 Stoddard Road
Modesto, CA 95352-3837
(800) 558-9595

National Foundation for Teaching Entrepreneurship
64 Fulton Street, Suite 700
New York, NY 10038
(212) 233-1777

Web Sites

For a great list of on-line craft sites, set your browser to: http://www.yahooligans.com/Art_Soup/crafts

Here's an interesting entrepreneurship education site: http://www.kidsway.com

This is a general crafts site for kids: http://www.makingfriends.com

Here's a site where people trade craft project ideas: http://www.geocities.com/EnchantedForest/3053/exchange

For beadwork projects take a look at this site: http://beadwork.miningco.com/msubkids.htm

There are many places to find clip art on the web. Here are a couple places to start: http://www.webplaces.com/html/clipart.htm and http://www.microsoft.com/clipgallerylive/eula.asp

NOTES

NOTES

NOTES

NOTES

NOTES